TOMATO IMPERATIVE!

TOMATO IMPERATIVE!

From Fried Green Tomatoes to
Summer's Ripe Bounty

Sharon Nimtz and Ruth Cousineau

Little, Brown and Company Boston New York Toronto London

First Edition

Library of Congress Cataloging-in-Publication Data
Nimtz, Sharon.
Tomato imperative!: fried green tomatoes to summer's ripe bounty:
more than 130 recipes for tomatoes, fresh and preserved / by
Sharon Nimtz and Ruth Cousineau. — 1st ed.
          p.   cm.
    Includes index.
    ISBN 0-316-60794-0
    1. Cookery (Tomatoes)   I. Cousineau, Ruth.   II. Title.
  TX803.T6N55   1994
  641.6'5642 — dc20   93-35618

10   9   8   7   6   5   4   3   2   1

MAR

*Published simultaneously in Canada
by Little, Brown & Company (Canada) Limited*

Printed in the United States of America

To our grandmothers,
Georgia
and
Sadie

A world without tomatoes is like a string quartet without violins. . . . In this world of uncertainty and woe, one thing remains unchanged: Fresh, canned, pureed, dried, salted, sliced and served with sugar and cream or pressed into juice, the tomato is reliable, friendly, and delicious. We would be nothing without it.

Laurie Colwin

Contents

CONTENTS

CONTENTS

Preface

*I*N THE SUMMER of 1991, after many years of enjoying others' efforts in the area of food newsletters, I decided to test the nuts-and-bolts of foodletterdom myself by putting together one issue on the subject of tomatoes. To myself I cited the precedent of the doyenne of English food writers, Elizabeth David, who had self-published at least one single-subject pamphlet.

If I learned from my effort, and if the results could in any way be interpreted as successful, I would turn them into a quarterly subscription newsletter, following the path forged in this wilderness by people whose work I admired very much indeed — people like John Thorne, out of Castine, Maine, whose *Simple Cooking* newsletter addresses the subject of food in ways that are witty, intelligent, diligent, iconoclastic. Edward Behr, up in Peacham, Vermont, writes a scholarly food letter called *The Art of Eating,* in which he explores ingredients, preparations, and ideas in a fascinating depth I had only experienced in Elizabeth David's work. Ed pointed me to *Food History News* and Karyl Bannister's *Cook & Tell* newsletter, both from Maine. From there I'd learned of Karen Hess — the definer of food history scholarship — and of John Martin Taylor down in Charleston, the expert on the Lowcountry and Gullah food lines to which I had been attracted by Vertamae Smart-Grosvenor's National Public Radio narratives.

As I sat down to the keyboard, we'd had our first greasy, salty, and tangy taste of fried green tomatoes and were waiting for the first peak-season ripe one. Appreciation and anticipation whetted my descriptive skills, and it was no trouble at all to gather up more than thirty recipes, techniques, history, lore, and reminiscence regarding the vegetable, er, ah, fruit . . . umm, berry (to be exact). *Tomato Imperative!* sold nicely through my weekly columns in the *Rutland* (Vermont) *Herald* and by word-of-mouth, but before I could seriously consider putting out another issue events conspired to keep me from it.

The fact that I'd sent a few copies of that original *Tomato Imperative!* to a few other food writers completely slipped my mind until the next June, when Florence Fabricant called from the *New York Times*. The favorable write-up of *T.I.!* in her "Food Notes" column started off an exhilarating chain of events. Through Karyl Bannister I became acquainted with John Tanasychuk, who wrote about *T.I.!* in his "Eating Well" column in the *Detroit Free Press*. That was picked up by the Knight-Ridder news service and appeared in newspapers all over the country. Sharon Sanders at the *Chicago Sun-Times* called to interview me for an article that ran with a photograph provided by my friend the photographer Michael Aleshire. One of the first respondents to the Fabricant article was Joni Miller, editor of the James Beard Foundation newsletter, who tipped off John and Matt Lewis Thorne, from whom I received a note asking would I please send a copy for mention in their *new* newsletter, *CookBook: The Food Book Review for Cooks Who Read.* I was flattered. Then, a few months later, Joni called me with the request to speak at the Beard Foundation's annual — and enormously popular — tomato-tasting event. "Er, ah, gulp," said this country writer. "Sure."

Meanwhile, a thousand orders flowed into my mailbox here in Vermont, well into the winter, from readers around the United States and beyond, many of whom proclaimed the excellence of their state's tomatoes — the most chauvinist of these were New Jerseyites and Michiganders. The letters and orders continue to this writing, putting new meaning into going to the post office.

By then, I was putting together a book proposal at the request of editors who had queried my willingness to do so. I was willing, but although my avocation for food and cooking is passionate, my vocation is in research and writing about those subjects. I called upon Ruth Cousineau, whom I was fortunate to have as a friend and neighbor.

Well-respected in the food world, Ruth had refined an impeccable food sense through her involvement in many prestigious undertakings over the years. These included owning and operating her own restaurant and working as a professional corporate chef and manager for an international corporation. In addition, time spent in France had prepared her to act as a translator and recipe tester for well-known cookbook authors and food magazines.

Both Ruth and I had been bred with a fascination with food as children at the knees of grandmothers, but what different grandmothers, and what different childhoods!

Ruth grew up in urban New York in an artistic and verbal family, with summers spent in and out of her grandma Sadie's kosher hotel kitchen in a little town called Sharon Springs in the northern Catskills (where her future husband, Len Cousineau, lived unsuspected all those years). She absorbed her passion for food and cooking watching her mother prepare the Jewish dishes of their heritage, and at her grandmother's knee as she cooked for family and a spa-hotel full of guests.

Even later, when for practical purposes she studied nursing, Ruth never deviated from that passion, but it was the time she and Len spent in Paris that brought cooking to mind as a career. Their daughter, Luce, was a toddler, and their son, Simon, was born there. "Living in Europe really affected us," she says. "The French respect food, they know how to treat it. The merchants don't cut cheese into little pieces and wrap it in plastic, they know cheese has life, and they cut a wedge fresh from the wheel for each patron, just as herbs are fresh cut to stand in cool water, and garlic isn't refrigerated!"

My childhood was spent on Michigan farms, absorbing the atmosphere of the midday dinners that my grandmother Georgia and other female kin prepared for harvesters and the eighteen-hour marathon canning days that were so necessary then.

Everything that happens on a farm has to do with food, and nurturing, of course, although both preoccupations remain largely unspoken. When I daydreamed my way barefoot down the sand-silky lane to "get the cows," I wasn't thinking about milk or cheese or cream, but I took for granted that big pail of house milk that Grandfather swung inside the kitchen door each evening after milking. The mysterious barn itself offered barrels of molasses and cakes of salt that, although meant for the cows, tasted good to my little brother and me, too. As I write, I can feel the striated marble surface of the salt-lick on my tongue.

In the way of young people through the ages, I suppose, it was not until I grew up and had my own family that I began to cherish my early food memories and to extend them, turning my writing skills to chef and restaurant reviews, reading M.F.K. Fisher and Elizabeth David and James Beard, developing a passionate interest in the welfare of small farms, and *cooking*.

Our mutual friend Susan Farrow had introduced Ruth and me some years before — "You two should know each other," she said, and took us to lunch. Ever since, we'd been looking for a project to involve us both, and *Tomato Imperative!* — the book — seemed to be it.

By November 1992, we had completed the proposal and, to our pleasure, acquired Meg Ruley as our agent and Jennifer Josephy of Little, Brown as our editor and publisher. I'd met Meg some years before, and determined that one day I would need an agent and she would be it. Jennifer's was the first letter I opened the day after the Fabricant article appeared, in which she said she was "smitten" with tomatoes. How could we resist?

Andrew Smith, tomato historian, was enormously and generously helpful with this book's tomato history, in spite of being in the process of publishing his own book, *The Tomato in America: Early History, Culture and Cookery* (1994), published by the University of South Carolina Press. Ed Behr was also generous with advice in correspondence with me.

One name and food-related enterprise led to another and then to another in this astonishing network I've been describing. Hoppin' John's Culinary Bookstore, in Charleston, is the enterprise of John Taylor (who published his own book in 1992, the excellent and definitive *Hoppin' John's Lowcountry Cooking*). He directed me to Nach Waxman's Kitchen Arts & Letters Bookstore and Gallery in New York City . . . and on and on.

Without exception, the loose-knit group of writers and scholars and businesspeople I've mentioned here were generous with their help, advice, and direction, passing me from one to the next, and I cannot thank them enough.

Making a book is a long and involved process, and when you're in Vermont, much of that process takes place a couple hundred miles away; you almost forget it is going on. It had been a long time in the making when we received the manuscript back from Betsy Pitha, our copy editor. She accompanied it with a warm and gracious letter that told of the pleasure she took in working on our book. We soon realized, as we went through the corrected manuscript, that Betsy was a woman with a mind like a well-oiled machine, which could connect page 43 with pages 443 and 575, meanwhile dealing with every aspect of the bibliography, differing name spellings, and the book as a whole. It was a fine balancing act that tied up all the loose ends of the manuscript with efficiency and style. Thank you, Betsy!

Our heartfelt gratitude must go to our families — Ralph, Isobel, and Len deserve thanks for their patience and for eating so many tomatoes this year, with not one complaint. Thanks must go to our friends and other relations who also ate a lot of tomatoes, besides lending us their moral support, their recipes, and their cooking and proofing skills: my mother, Beth Parquette, Ruth's mother-in-law, Mary Cousineau, Chris Powers, Marilyn Thomas, Kathleen Murphy Patten, Sandy and Dale Lincoln, Jane Quigley, Peder and Linda Johnson, Carol Bliss Macleod, Andy and Chris Anderson Snyder, Justin and Gale Courcelle, Angela Combes, Esther Cohen, François Dinand, Betty Stewart, Joyce Barbieri, Dana and Jeremy Squire, Sharon Pressly and her mother, Pat Lipstreu, and Ron Holdridge, my correspondent from Japan.

Other cooks, writers, and friends who have aided and abetted with their kindness are Janet Greene, Konstantin and Soo Schonbachler, Deedy Marble, Jasper White, Ken Haedrich, Eugene Walter, and Elizabeth Alston. And thanks to our suppliers of ingredients and thought — Lisa Lorimer of Vermont Bread Company, Jim Reiman of Sweet Tomatoes Trattorias, Al Shep of Al Ducci's, Justin Rashid at American Spoon Foods, Black River Produce, Ellen Lev and her mother, Reba Pressman, from Stonehill Farms, and Larry Lipman of 6L Packing Company.

And to everyone involved with the culinary collection at the Schlesinger Library at Radcliffe, including the parking attendant at the Divinity School; and to the *Rutland Herald,* we say thank you.

Nowadays, Ruth and Len live in Clarendon, Vermont, in the brick Federal that once was home to their restaurant, surrounded by herbs and flowers and a pond filled with goldfish the size of trout. She cooks for and counsels at Spring Lake Ranch, a residential treatment community for emotionally and mentally disturbed adults. Her children are grown and cooking for themselves.

I live with my husband, Ralph, and our youngest child, Isobel, and sometimes Spencer, our firstborn, in the neighboring community of Wallingford, in a brick colonial on a corner lot that thinks it's a farm. I too, of course, have my herb gardens, but, sadly, no cows. I write freelance articles about food and regular food columns.

A love of food — it comes from childhood, and once felt never lessens.

TOMATO IMPERATIVE!

Introduction

The Herb Garden

One of the most sensuous culinary pleasures is to wander out into the yard at suppertime to gather snippets of the leaves and flowers that add color, aroma, and flavor to the foods we are preparing. The soft greens, grays, silvers, and blues of most herbal foliage, many with tiny flowers, make them a treat to grow even if they were not aromatic and flavorful in culinary use. They can be bought dried, and increasingly they are available more or less fresh in the supermarket, but the most satisfactory way of acquiring them is by growing them — in windowsill pots, in patio crevices, or in the garden proper. For the most part they require little care besides sowing a few seeds or planting a little pot of them in a corner — handy to the kitchen — of not extraordinarily rich soil that gets

Food Nostalgia in the Age of Supermarkets

NOSTALGIA for real food — for the ripe heft of it, its twiny odors, speckled still with dirt from the field, and even difficult with hoary roots and fronds — is abundant in the nation. The rare, fresh, real taste of it evokes memory — trickle of sweat in the heat of midday picking, prickle of vine and spine, slither of snake in berry bog, spicy-hot smell of summer field, space of insect-humming noon, sound of distant, ghostly call of mourning doves in the cool dew of a strawberry morning, sheer terror and racing adrenaline of dank November butchering dawn, father's edgy excitement at season's first morel hunt, and grandmother's floury hands as she fits lard-white pastry into scalloped-edge Pyrex. All these intensify our own satisfaction when we manage to create a space in the workday in which to prepare a lunch for friends. From scratch. But when we bring back pale, denatured food from supermarkets we miss everything but the sheer getting-by of food. In the plastic and Styrofoam of pork chops, death and supper become anonymous, and in the cotton non-taste of store-bought tomatoes there is reason to start a garden.

Needing Gardens

The simple little self-sufficient garden is the microcosm now of our agrarian past, the answer to these longings for real food. A close acquaintance with growing things has become again a reassurance in an uncertain world, perhaps in direct relation to the number of years a person has spent in it. In our twenties we acted with instinct, scrabbling away the sod, planting the peas, lettuce, and tomatoes. Why? I could not tell you even then, only that I grew up with this kind of behavior (and seriously tried to ignore it) and there it was — spring, and time for human beings to put seeds into the ground to grow food and flowers. Ten years later, onward and upward, we zealously cultivated bigger and better, and more and more varied, learning that what we had considered "foreign" — cilantro, fava beans, radicchio, all manner of herbs — would grow perfectly well in our own gardens and satisfy our senses and our needs much more fully than would supermarket produce.

Nowadays, we're selective, growing only the tenderest peas, the crunchiest, most colorful, and tastiest leafy things, and the most flavorful but not necessarily the best-looking tomatoes, along with beans, okra, fennel, leeks, eggplant, and peppers — produce that we cannot easily find here in other gardens and local markets, or that, if available commercially, have lost the flavor they retain only until picking. We look forward to the gardening season as a relief from the indoors, from intentional aerobics, from stale intellectual endeavor, from, finally, sleeping too much in our winter-foolish hibernation. Gardening is a treat and a relaxation for the senses — each and every one of them — and at the end there is food, glorious, beautiful, pure food redolent of its own flesh, good dirt, and open air.

We're not alone in this. Probably more than half of the households in this country have some sort of vegetable garden, to grow at least the tomato, if only in a pot on the patio or trailing down a window ledge six stories up. And the reason is simple. To go into the garden among the green-smelling tomato vines, to heft the round plumpness of the perfectly ripe tomato gently in the palm of your hand, to close your fingers around its glossy stretched skin and to tip it — just tip it from its stem so that it falls heavily, released into your cupped hand — is no small pleasure, but one whose magnitude sustains us through other seasons and less pleasant tasks and tastes. No other vegetable is anticipated with such intensity, cherished for its quality and pro-

some sun. Among the perennials that are the first living green things to venture out shoots in our chilly Vermont gardens each year are tarragon, sorrel, mint, onion and garlic chives, Egyptian onions, sage, wild ginger, lovage, and lavender. Tiny leaves of thyme reappear or renew, imperceptibly, on old stems, chervil reseeds itself, as does dill, and biennial parsley is a spring treat and can be picked, along with sage and sometimes thyme, almost the whole year through. If it has been planted the fall before, garlic will sprout early and can be used for greens and for the immature bulb as well as the mature, cloven bulb. Each year we plant nasturtiums and pots and pots of basil, as well as regular sowings of cilantro and arugula. A pot of rosemary is planted and pinched for dinners throughout the summer, then repotted or pulled up by its roots to dry, to be used throughout the winter. In fact, many of the herbs can be hung in bunches and dried, to provide good flavor throughout the winter.

Rodale's Illustrated Encyclopedia of Herbs is one good and comprehensive reference. Other interesting ones are The Complete Medicinal Herbal, by Penelope Ody, and Hints & Pinches, by Eugene Walter.

fusion at this one time of year and for its serendipitous match-making with eggplant, red pepper, okra, onion, leek, garlic, and herbs in sumptuous, healthy, varied meals. Suddenly there is scant reason to attend the supermarket or the butcher.

A Short, Amateur History of the Fruit

The history of the tomato is circuitous and opaque, and there are people who devote their lives to discovering it. If it is difficult for the uninitiated to weed among the disagreements to find the fruit of truth, it is no less difficult for the experts to discover it in the first place.

In the first issue of *Tomato Imperative!* I wrote, "The very earliest tomatoes, back into prehistory, were weedy pests that invaded the maize and bean fields in Central America. Eventually the natives began to harvest the weeds as well as the maize. It was a healthy choice, for the tomato provided vitamins, missing from maize, which discouraged pellagra." I wrote innocently, ignorantly, trusting the written word that had told me this, liking this neat, round theory.

I sent a copy to Edward Behr, a food scholar in the northern part of our state, asking his opinion. "Are you sure," he sent back, "that your word 'prehistory' is quite correct in this context? And the weeds-in-the-corn sounds a little pop. Any good citations?"

I only knew what I'd read, and so, apparently, did the food historians before me. Still, I was aghast that my lack of scholarship was helping to disseminate pseudo-facts.

I had continued: "When Cortés arrived in the early 1500s he found the natives shaving the green fruit they called *tomatl* into many of their dishes, while the ripe, probably yellow fruit was made into a sauce along with hot chile peppers to be eaten with beans."

"Almost all tomato lore is inaccurate, or false," Andrew Smith, a contemporary historian, wrote to me. "For instance, you note that Cortés found green tomatoes in Mexico. I know of no original source which supports this, although many people have made the claim."

Apparently, the problem was linguistic. The Aztecs called both the tomatillo and the tomato by the Nahuatl word *tomatl*, which means merely "something plump," says Smith. The Spanish were confused and called both *tomate*. Still, it would seem that anyone shaving a three-quarter-inch tomatillo into a stew would need to have a mighty small knife.

A tomatillo, by the way, is only very distantly related to the tomato, which is of the family *Solanaceae,* whose members include belladonna, black henbane, and deadly nightshade, and that might explain why, through much of its history, the tomato was thought to be unwholesome. Or perhaps it was common to eat the leaves as well as the fruit, before it was known that the leaves are not deadly but certainly toxic.

From my further study and talk with generous scholars what does seem certain is that the tomato originated in the northern arm of the Andes, in Peru, Ecuador, Chile, beside the mountains and along the coast. It may have traveled to Central America through the centuries, although it is still a mystery why it was not often the subject of drawings on pottery and other artifacts. It is quite probable that Hernando Cortés took seeds of the tomato back to Spain with him after his ruthless and barbaric conquest of Mexico, and it is possible that the slave-trading Portuguese took them to Africa in the subsequent century. Perhaps the Africans took to the fruit with little hesitation, and there is some conjecture that some of the African people impressed into slavery brought tomato seeds with them, in some form, when they were brought to this continent. They, then, would have introduced the tomato to the South.

Others say that the Spanish introduced the tomato to Florida and then to New Orleans at least by 1797. Whichever route it took, from Florida it found its way very slowly up the East Coast, and from New Orleans it traveled north on the Mississippi. But, particularly in the northern states, among isolated people, the fruit was believed to be unwholesome at the very least, and was used only as an ornamental.

The Tomato

A whole tomato fresh from the garden, eaten raw, juice running down your chin and over your paws, will most likely weigh 5 to 8 ounces, have about 27 calories, 1.4 grams of protein, 6 grams of carbohydrate, .6 grams of fiber, .2 grams of fat, 1,100 International Units of vitamin A, 28 of vitamin C, rags and tags of the B vitamins, a little bit of iron, 16 milligrams of calcium, 33 of phosphorus, 4 of sodium, and 300 of potassium.

For our purposes a large tomato weighs 7 to 8 ounces (although some Beefsteaks can weigh a pound or up to 3 pounds); a medium one 4 to 5 ounces, and a small one 3 ounces.

One large tomato, peeled, seeded, and chopped, will measure about ⅔ cup. Coarsely chopped with the skin, seeds, and juice, one large tomato will equal about 1 cup.

Store tomatoes stem side up, never in the refrigerator.

What Is This Thing Called Tomato?

In Europe the first known mention of the tomato was in the Italian Pier Andrea Mattioli's herbal in 1544. He likened it to mandrake, a plant believed to be poisonous, whose roots were said to resemble a man's legs and to screech when pulled from the earth. *Mala insana,* he called it, unhealthy fruit. Nevertheless, there is some evidence that Italian and Spanish cooks were using tomatoes by 1544. The English, however, grew it as an ornamental for two centuries before eating it. In 1636, the second edition of Gerard's *Herball* called it the Apple of Love, and said it "bringeth forth very long round stalkes or branches, fat and full of juice, trailing upon the ground, not able to sustain himselfe upright by reason of the tendernesse of the stalkes, and also the great weight of the leaves and fruit," which was described as "chamfered, uneven, and bunched out in many places; of a bright shining red colour, and the bignesse of a goose egge or a large pippin. . . . The whole plant is of a ranke and stinking savour." Gerard mentioned that it grew in "Spaine, Italie, and such hot countries, from whence my selfe have received seeds for my garden, where they doe increase and prosper."

In the sixteenth century, botanists assigned it the Latin name of *Lycopersicon* (wolf peach) — not because it looked good enough to eat, but because it was thought to resemble Galen's description of *Lycopersicon* in his Roman herbal. It is now officially *Lycopersicon esculentum* — edible wolf peach.

Back home, Thomas Jefferson planted the tomato in 1781, but John Martin Taylor notes that it was grown in Charleston for food as early as 1764. By the 1840s, after formidable amounts of persuasion on the part of interested persons, it had become a fashionable crop even in the North. Campbell's soup cannery was built in 1869, requiring that in the 1870s the tomato become a commercial crop, and the rest is history.

The tomato is technically a berry, and certainly a fruit, which is a structure that develops from the ovary of the plant as the result of fertilization. A vegetable is some part of an herb or plant that is edible, like the carrot's root or the spinach's leaf.

In 1893, the United States Supreme Court ruled that because the tomato was used as a vegetable — eaten with the main part of the meal instead of at the end — it should be legally classified as such, and therefore be subject to tariffs when imported from abroad. And so it remains, much to the delight of commercial growers in this country.

Breeding

There is conjecture and quite a bit of certainty that the tomato was bred for improvements for over 2,000 years by sophisticated pre-Columbian civilizations. Common sense tells us they bred first for taste, then perhaps for size, disease resistance, maybe even for transportation, but that would not have been first priority. That would have been flavor.

Once the tomato as we know it began to be in demand in large numbers by canneries, and in winter by people from the North, it began to be bred for uniformity (easier to pack), tough skin and firmness (for long-distance jostling), and a jointless joining to the stem (easier machine picking). It was even bred slightly square, to make it more compliant on a conveyor belt. What is missing here? Oh, right, flavor. Well.

Flavor develops slowly, as the photosynthesis of a well-leafed plant produces sugars, acids, and aromatic oils to nurture the young fruit over a long period of time. Once the fruit leaves the plant, the production of flavor ceases abruptly. When tomatoes are picked green for transport, they are blasted at a certain point with ethylene gas, which is the reddening agent naturally produced by tomatoes and other fruit, to jump-start their own release of the gas just in time to look pretty in the supermarket. In spite of this, winter tomatoes are not merely green tomatoes colored red, as you would think. Mysteriously, they do not taste green. Natural, immature green tomatoes out of the garden are firm, even crisp, and juicy, with a sour clean taste that is useful and delicious in many preparations. Supermarket tomatoes are grainy in texture, with a pale, insipid taste.

We seldom buy so-called fresh tomatoes out of season, unless there are good plum tomatoes available. An exception, if we could find them, are the tomatoes that one or two companies follow from Florida in the winter to New Jersey in the summer, and then back again. Alas, these never-gassed, never-refrigerated, always sun-ripened tomatoes are available only to select chefs and greengrocers at a very dear price.

Since the tomato is second in farm value only to the potato — we Americans spend more than $2.5 billion on fresh tomatoes per year — the person(s) who can make it winter-palatable and in demand will make a pretty penny. I myself have no more faith in the new genetic engineering process that will supposedly allow a tomato to ripen flavorfully on the vine yet remain firm enough to ship than anyone should who grew up in the postwar, petrochemical era. Are we so sure that food is not so inextricably bound with its begetting and getting that without the hunt, the sweat, the total experience, we will find that it has lost a good part of its power to sustain, and to nurture?

We hope that you have a small plot of land or even a flowerpot or two in which to grow your own vine-ripened tomatoes. At least one or two, to taste, to remember what the real thing is, after all.

How It Grows Best

It is sowne in the beginning of Aprill in a bed of hot horse-dung, after the maner of muske Melons and such like cold fruits.

John Gerard, *Herball*

I was startled to hear it suggested recently that we northerners were not the best fitted for growing tomatoes or anything else that couldn't be grown by planting seeds directly into the garden. This is taking *natural* a bit far. Whatever one person can do without the help of multinational corporations and still obtain satisfactory results is what I consider natural.

Here in this cold little state, the earlier you get your seeds started, the more self-sufficiently correct you are considered to be. "Got your tomatoes started?" people begin asking in January, when mailboxes burst with seed catalogs. By Town Meeting Day, for which the first Tuesday in March is designated, they were shocked when I told them no. No, no, no. We want to get them started eight weeks before our traditional garden-planting weekend — Memorial Day — after which we sincerely hope and can vaguely trust that a frost won't occur. That would be April 1, which I know seems rather late, but I was heartened to read the comments of my across-the-mountain neighbor, seedsman Shep Ogden, in an article by Anne Raver in the *New York Times,* who said he'd been putting his seeds in later and later, just from laziness (and this, really, is how I come to my own wisdom), until now he has decided that the second week in April is good. Any earlier, and they get stressed out before the soil warms up to at least fifty degrees, start worrying that they're going to die, and duly decide to have babies. In other words, they take steps to propagate the species, to be the fittest, and so to survive.

Just after I got my seeds started, my friend Dana called from Virginia, worried that she had not been able to get into her garden because it had been raining! "It's so late," she said, truly concerned. It took me a while, but as I gazed out of my window onto the debris of a late snowstorm, something snapped, and I said, "Now hold on there. If I can grow a garden up here starting on Memorial Day, surely you can start one down there sometime in April or May. As a matter of fact, you can start two in the time it takes my tomatoes to ripen." In the Lowcountry section of South Carolina, there are two tomato seasons — one in June and the other in November.

In my old, low-light brick house I start the seeds on top of the refrigerator — the only place it's warm here — covered with plastic. When they start bumping their little heads, I gradually uncover them and put them in a west-facing office window under Vitalites, which may or may not help tomatoes' growth or humans' seasonal depression. When I finally plant them out, they are short and stocky, like bulls, and they positively shoot up. Everyone else's plants are a foot taller, but I get tomatoes just as early, and just as good, maybe better.

The best tomatoes come from indeterminate plants, which means that they keep growing longer stems, more branches and leaves, and setting fruit until they are killed by frost. Because they have more leaves, these plants do more photosynthesizing, which means they make more food to feed the fruit. The leaves also protect it from extremes of temperature. Determinate plants stop growing at a certain point and set all their fruit at once. So there you are, first canning yourself to death to take care of the plethora, then buying fresh tomatoes from your neighbor because yours have gone by. Late tomatoes have much more flavor than early ones because the fruits have more time to grow, to develop, to become totally delicious. Also, strains that produce fewer fruits, like some heirlooms, will have better flavor because the plants are putting more energy into flavor than into reproduction.

I have never had a bit of trouble growing tomatoes, even the year they didn't go in until the Fourth of July, but that garden, new to me, was on the site of an ancient chicken yard. Bonanza! The best tomatoes, it seems to me, have grown in hot summers that were dry when the fruits were forming. I see the sandy Michigan garden, so flat it looks concave, with that bowl of pale blue sky over it. It produced fat, juicy tomatoes to swear by, and many Michiganders do.

In our Vermont garden, we use goat manure and our own compost and this year a little lime to sweeten and balance the nitrogen. Sometimes, but seldom, we plant and dig under a green manure like winter rye. I never pinch, and used not to stake, only to spread a good layer of newspapers beneath the branches. Now we surround the plants with fat, breezy barrels made of 6-inch fencing. So, if you set out plants that have buds but not flowers, that are stocky but not leggy, and don't worry if they suffer a little bit from low moisture, high heat, and only a moderately rich soil, it all seems to intensify the flavor.

In your own garden, grow flavorful, delicate, juicy tomatoes and skip the varieties that are bred to toughness in order to survive transport or conveyor belts. Beefsteaks are among the most tasty. We also like Abraham Lincoln, Better Boy, Brandywine, Celebrity, as well as Carmello, Burbank, Super Marmande, San Marzano for sauce, Principe Borghese for drying. I know some people care how their tomatoes look, but I find any of them beautiful when they taste good.

A translucent skin over red flesh equals pink tomatoes. Yellow tomatoes are as acid as red, and tomatoes that are advertised as "low-acid" usually have not less acid but more sugars. The meatiest tomatoes have the least amount of gel and seeds and so are the least acid.

Some people believe they are allergic to tomatoes. And some do, indeed, develop a rash after eating tomatoes. But tomatoes are cleansing agents, and the rash may consist of impurities that the fruit is dislodging. I knew a little girl forty years ago who was allergic to tomatoes. Every year, in the second or third week of tomato season, she would break out in a terrific rash. It was so bad that she was obliged to miss her piano recital, which, unfortunately, always took place just at that time.

The Recipe

What is a recipe but documentation of an improvisation? But on what is that improvisation based? It is based on how things have been done, on history and availability, and on what our grandmothers did. It is based on nostalgia and sophistication, discovery, creative common sense and, yes, even invention on top of knowledge. I am musing on this as I nibble on a leaf of endive used as a shovel for salmon that was roasted last night and today has been mashed with seasonings and aromatics and bound together with a mayonnaise incorporating Dried Tomato Harissa. It is as improvisational as Ella Fitzgerald's scat or Dagwood's sandwich, and it is delicious.

Sometimes something happens in a recipe that you can't imagine by reading it; a certain reaction, between two ingredients or the ingredients and technique, creates something entirely different from what you had anticipated. We came across an old Shaker recipe for sweet tomato dumplings that sounded odious until we remembered an apple dumpling recipe in which cored apples are stuffed with sugar and cinnamon, the whole wrapped in pastry, stood in a baking dish, syrup poured around, and baked. You would think the pastry would be damp and unattractive, but instead it is crisp and puffed — a wonderful dish. That's why we like to try a recipe just as it is, in order to give ourselves the chance to say, "Oh, this is what they meant," before going about changing it and making it our own.

The recipes that follow are ones we've been preparing for years, as well as those given us by friends and family, and those we found in our hours of scrabbling through old books. We sought them ethnically and historically and finally seasonally, always guided by our taste buds, and then we filled in with those that did not seem to exist but, according to our sensibilities, should. We took a good gander at the ones we found, asked ourselves where they would have originated, from whom and why, should they be made more contemporary, and how could they be improved. We've arranged them seasonally, according to the calendar, with a preponderance of green tomato recipes fore and aft and sprinkled in between, then in peak garden season making use of other fresh garden vegetables, full of summer flavor, sparked with tastes of fresh herbs.

One of the biggest pleasures we had in making this book was finding recipes using green tomatoes, adapting recipes to use green tomatoes, or, unapologetically, inventing them, because this woefully underutilized fruit, cold, sour, clean, and crisp, is as much a food as red, and melds so nicely with buttermilk, cilantro, and apples. They're tougher, harder walled, and they can do with a bit of pre-sautéing, steaming, or simply salting to draw out some of the liquid and soften the walls, and they sometimes like a touch of sugar — not a lot or the sugar and the tomato will put on boxing gloves — but a bit to tame them subtly.

Eugene Walter, novelist, poet, essayist, who was consultant to the food stylist on the movie *Fried Green Tomatoes,* told me that the way southern recipes are written is with the ingredients one will no doubt have to buy listed first, followed by what one *probably* has in the kitchen, followed by what one *surely* has in the kitchen, such as flour. But we've listed our ingredients strictly in order of use.

"My mother," Ruth says, "always says to me, 'I made this great veal and pepper dish, but I didn't have veal so I used chicken, and I didn't have peppers so I used . . .' " However, if you want to know what we liked about the dish to include it here, we suggest making it by the letter first, and next time improvising.

. . . only two things
that money can't buy,
and that's True Love
and Home Grown Tomatoes . . .
True love, and Home Grown tomatoes . . .

Song written and sung by Guy Clark

Techniques

Cracking: For coarse seeds and peppercorns, lean on a heavy cast-iron frying pan placed over them; twist it a bit if necessary. For long-cooked dishes, or to give strong bursts of flavor, crushing or bruising seeds slightly releases the flavors.

Grinding: Put seeds, spices, and/or nuts that have been roasted and cooled into a sturdy mortar and pound with a pestle. Small amounts of nuts may be ground in a blender or chopped fine in a food processor, but seeds and spices get lost in these machines.

To grind seeds or spices in a coffee grinder: Whir small pieces of sturdy bread in the grinder to clean it. Discard the bread and whir the seeds or spices until they are powder. This is good for grinding a few days' worth of peppercorns. You can clean the coffee grinder of the remains of the aromatic seeds by the bread method (remembering that there are worse things than cumin- or caraway- or even black-pepper-scented coffee in the morning).

Juicing: Squeeze halved tomatoes gently.

Pureeing: Chunk raw tomatoes (green or red) into the bowl of a food processor, whir, then put through a food mill to remove seeds and skins. One pound of tomatoes yields 1⅔ cups of tomato puree. If skin and seeds are not a problem, forget about the food mill.

Roasting: Roasting seeds, whole spices, and nuts refreshes the volatile oils, which renews flavors and aromas, and is well worth the few minutes and the bit of care it takes. To do it, toss and toast in a small, heavy-bottomed pan over low heat until the aromas are released, or place in a 350-degree oven for 5 to 10 minutes. Watch carefully, as they burn easily. Cool before using.

Roasting Tomatoes: See p. 19 for this technique.

Salting: To draw out excess liquids and/or bitterness from green and red tomatoes, eggplant, or cabbage, sprinkle liberally with coarse salt, let drain at least 15 minutes, then rinse and pat dry with kitchen towels.

Seeding: To seed a tomato, cut in half horizontally and gently squeeze, or hook your little finger into each chamber to pull out the seeds and most of the gel with it.

Skinning: To peel a tomato, plunge it into boiling water for 10 seconds. Drain. Rinse in cold water and slip off the skin. To peel a pepper, use a swivel-bladed vegetable parer. Halve and seed, then turn skin side down and, with a sharp flexible knife blade at just a short angle, slice the membranes from the inside of the pepper. This method is suitable for peppers when they will be cooked.

To skin or peel peppers for salads: Grill or broil the entire surface of the red pepper until the skin blisters and blackens, then remove it from the fire, put it on a plate to catch any juices, and toss a kitchen towel over it for a few minutes to let the steam loosen the blackened skin from the flesh. After the pepper has steamed under the towel and is handleable, remove the skin with your fingers, core and remove seeds, and proceed with the recipe. If you are working with a whole red pepper, the juices will remain inside. Or broil halves or quarters on an ovenproof plate to catch juices.

Slicing: Unless you *want* onion rings, slice an onion in half through the stem and root end, then slice each half lengthwise, to end up with shards rather than rounds. These long shards can then be sliced crosswise into the size desired. They cook better this way and are not as disconcerting to pull out of, say, a stir-fry or a soup as is a floppy ring.

Smashing: For garlic, shallots, gingerroot, olives: peel garlic and shallots easily by placing the flat of a wide knife blade or Chinese cleaver over them and giving it a whack with the side of your fist. Pick off the papery skin and cut off the root end. No garlic presses for us — most of the garlic seems to stay in the press, and besides, we can never find one when we need it. If, instead, you crush the garlic, you need do nothing more to it. Use this method with rounds of fresh gingerroot too, but mince them a bit more if necessary. But just lean on a wide flat blade placed over olives of all kinds, one at a time, to make the pit accessible through the flesh. Then pit them with your fingers.

Weighing: We weigh almost everything, using a small, inexpensive Krups or Braun scale. My grandfather's grain-scoop Hanson hangs in my window for bigger jobs. Weighing things allows you to use a pound of any size tomatoes. I like to weigh flour because I don't like to sift (4 ounces of King Arthur Unbleached White equals 1 cup). Then I fluff it by stirring with a whisk.

Ingredients We Like to Use

Anchovies: We like to find the whole, small fish packed in salt in large, colorful tins. Once you open the can, pack the fish in a glass jar, cover tightly, and refrigerate. They'll keep for many months. To use, rinse the salt from the fish, pull off the back fin, separate the fillets, and pull out the backbone. These have a marvelous taste, totally unlike those metallic-tasting ones packed in the little cans. If you can't find salted anchovies, ones packed in glass in oil are the next best thing. As a rule, a whole anchovy equals about four of the fillets that are packed in oil.

Butter: Use unsalted, because it is sweeter and fresher, with a taste like fresh cream. Salt is used to preserve butter or to disguise an off weed the cows ate. If you miss the taste of salt, it is far tastier to spread your good bread with unsalted butter, then sprinkle with coarse salt. I remember crunching on the rare large crystal of salt in the butter my grandmother made. That was pretty delicious, let me tell you.

Capers: These are the pickled buds of the caper bush that add piquancy and a special zing to Mediterranean foods. Some people like the tiny ones labeled nonpareil, others like the gigantic salted ones sold by the handful in Italian groceries. To use, rinse them, pat them dry, then chop. Store in the refrigerator.

Chiles: All sizes, shapes, and flavors of chiles are becoming standard supermarket items, thanks to the popularity of ethnic, especially Mexican, foods. We use anchos, which are dried poblanos, and chipotles, which are smoke-dried jalapeños. Soak them before using, or merely chop them dry before adding to liquids. We use, as well, the fresh forms. This summer we are growing the fiery habanero, poblano, Chile Colorado, and New Mex Joe Parker. Each has a different flavor, which is intriguing, and a different degree of heat. See *The Whole Chile Pepper Book* by Dave DeWitt and Nancy Gerlach (Little, Brown, 1990). Be sure to wash your hands after handling hot peppers, or you can put an eye out! It'll feel like it, anyway.

Pure Vermont Maple Syrup: Each year we both like to get a gallon of Spring Lake Ranch's B-Grade syrup. We both think that B and even C, if you can get it, have much more maple flavor than Fancy, Medium, or Dark Amber, which, while admittedly very fine, lack the nice, peasanty, strong maple flavor of B or C.

Olives: Find a reputable store and experiment with sweet, oil-cured black Moroccans (inferior ones can be bitter); gaetas, marinated in wine to an evocative T; large, green, fresh Sicilians, which you crack and marinate yourself, or eat as is; and tiny, brothy piccolinis, green-tasting and buttery. Note: Be sure to warn your guests if you have not pitted the olives before incorporating them into the dish.

Olive Oil: Use a good, green extra-virgin olive oil with lots of flavor whenever the flavor will really show up. Because it's too expensive to use in every case, switch to a cheaper, more refined olive oil (or even canola) for cooking. Experiment with good Spanish, Greek, Italian, and French olive oils. Have a tasting!

Onions: As you will see, we use every member of the onion family — garlic, shallots, leeks (both domestic and the wild ramp), scallions, and onions of every hue — and we grow most of them too, including the walking, or Egyptian, onion because we like to use the stems as chives, and because we enjoy them as a perennial. We don't use elephant garlic because it's too mild.

Parmesan Cheese: Parmigiano Reggiano, the only authentic Parmesan, is made in Parma, Italy. It is expensive but worth it, as only a bit at a time imparts its distinctive, nutty flavor. The less expensive Asiago is an acceptable substitute, and Romano is sweeter, saltier, and also very good. Keep it wrapped first in waxed paper, then in plastic, and refrigerated. Grate it fresh for each use, or pare curls of it with a vegetable peeler.

Salt: We use a coarse salt, without additives, because we like to be able to taste it in the food, and because additives are rarely good for you, nor do they taste good. Beyond that, we are not sophisticated. Ed Behr, in his *Artful Eater,* has some delightful and sophisticated things to say about salt.

Sausages and Hams: Chorizo is a slightly spicy, half-cured Portuguese and Spanish sausage, which is not widely available in all parts of the country. Substitute Italian sweet sausage if you cannot find it. Smithfield ham is a very salty, flavorful, dry ham made in Virginia. It is similar to prosciutto, which is again available here. Slice either ham thin. It lasts forever.

A Note on Roasting Tomatoes

Oven-roasting tomatoes and other vegetables imbues them with a deep, rich flavor not found in pan-simmering. The roasting method keeps the whole process conveniently out of the way and the thickening sauce safely unscorchable since it is not on a direct heat. This technique is used in our recipes for Mary Cousineau's Herbed Tomato Juice (p. 77), Roasted Plain Tomato Sauce (p. 108), and Roasted Tomato and Vegetable Sauce (p. 110).

Not only does roasting intensify flavors, but all parts of the vegetable except the garden dirt can go into the pan — stems, cores, and seeds can add their flavor and come back out in the food mill afterward, although if it's a thick sauce we're after, we often do seed and juice the tomatoes to lessen the overall cooking time.

Sometimes we like to cook the tomatoes first, without stirring, on top of the stove until the excess colorless water is released and can be poured off to be used in soups or broths or to braise a fish. Then the tomatoes are put into a large roasting pan and roasted until done.

Roasted tomatoes can usually be pureed directly in a food mill; harder vegetables can be chopped briefly in the bowl of a food processor before putting them into the food mill.

We find it's easier to preserve small amounts of juice or sauce in available interstices of time — much less onerous and not at all dreadful to anticipate, especially if one lacks a large, extended family to help.

Part 1

In the Beginning Is Green

Everybody on the Gulf Coast giggled and gurgled when that mad girl Fannie Flagg published a book called *Fried Green Tomatoes at the Whistle Stop Cafe*. But when they heard there would be a film adapted from the book, two subjects dominated conversation: What would Hollywood call the film, and how did your Grammaw cook her fried green tomatoes?

Eugene Walter

OCCASIONALLY MY GRANDMOTHER WOULD come in from her Michigan garden wearing a little self-satisfied grin and cradling some green tomatoes in the pouch of her apron. In the kitchen she would slice them, dip them in egg, dredge them in crushed saltines, and fry them up in lard. The taste was good and greasy and salty, too, with a clean sourness that could pucker the roof of your mouth.

When I started writing about tomatoes a couple of years ago, it was pleasant to go out into my Vermont garden to follow Grandma's example, only I would use a coarse yellow cornmeal and a fragrant olive oil, and would fry some zucchini blossoms, which the kids love, and okra, which we have learned to grow and appreciate, along with them, and rest some basil leaves among the fried things so that we ate the sense of basil right along with everything else.

More than just the taste of them was a stab of something else, excitement, or nostalgia for a food we hadn't eaten since childhood. Evidently we were not alone in this nostalgia. One gray and sleety Sunday afternoon the following February, we saw the movie *Fried Green Tomatoes* and came away with a hankering that would not be satisfied until at least July of the following Vermont summer, for the green tomato is nothing if not a fruit of the season.

But there is much more to the subject of green tomatoes than frying them, and Eugene Walter, who lives in Mobile, is an expert. Frying tomatoes seems to have remained a southern technique, probably an African one, brought forth to utilize New World foods such as tomatoes and cornmeal and, from the ubiquitous pig, lard.

Up North, green tomatoes weren't so often fried as treated in the north-ern European manner. Ruth's grandmother was Polish and never fried a tomato in her life, but pickled them and made them into chutneys and mincemeat. Those are the recipes you will find in many old cookbooks. We've included a few that intrigued us in this book.

But we think that come early season or end of summer, people through the centuries have been tossing a few chopped green tomatoes into soups and stews, paella, risotto, and pasta sauces — depending upon their cul-ture of origin — without thinking about it too much or writing it down in a "receipt" to pass on to future generations. Although there is a danger that as people spend less time learning from their elders, this kind of unwritten wisdom will disappear from culinary practice, without even thinking about it we invented green tomato dishes all by ourselves, through necessity (see Grilled Pale Vegetable Casserole, p. 33). We have learned what the native Americans whom Cortés observed knew — that ripeness is not all when it comes to tomatoes, although it is an inordinately pleasant stage. We use green tomatoes first because we can't wait for them to turn red, at season's end because there are so many of them, and always because they are good, their flavor and uses completely their own. So let's start with a scattering of green things in this season, then look ahead to the Last Green Tomatoes chapter.

Fried Green Tomatoes

Fried Green Tomatoes and Variations

𝓜AKE a private treat for yourself of a fried green tomato in the middle of a hot summer day. Take the plate of slices with a big napkin and a good book out to the hammock, and if there's anyone else around, particularly children, even picky eaters, pretty soon they'll come nedging along and asking, "Whatchoo doin'? Whazzat yer eatin' . . . all 'lone?" And then they'll want a taste, and then you'll have to get up and fry another tomato. You can fry them in flour or cracker crumbs, but we prefer cornmeal or semolina.

A platter of these with zucchini blossoms, okra, and eggplant treated in the same way is a real treat! Salt the eggplant slices and allow to drain for half an hour before proceeding. Tuck nasturtiums (flowers and leaves) and spriglets of basil leaves among the fried things for added zest and beauty. In a little gem of a book, *Cooking by the Garden Calendar,* Ruth Matson suggests serving fried tomatoes with individual corn custards and a white sauce, made out of the leftover frying butter, a bit of flour, and cream, to be poured over the tomatoes. Eugene Walter suggests frying in a mixture of oil and bacon fat, and he likes to use celery seed and dillweed, particularly dried, in the flour binder. Another time, he suggests using truly hard green tomatoes and coating them with mayonnaise before dipping into toasted crumbs. Still another time, we like to slice green tomatoes thick, sprinkle with salt, brush with garlicky olive oil, and grill them as

a tart, salty accompaniment to grilled meats. But this is the way
we do it first.

Serves 4

4 large green tomatoes
  just blushed with
  pink
2 large eggs
2 tablespoons milk
1 cup semolina or
  cornmeal

2 teaspoons salt
several grinds of pepper
2 to 4 tablespoons olive
  oil
2 to 4 tablespoons butter

Cut the tomatoes into thick slices and discard the ends. Beat
the eggs lightly with the milk. On a large piece of waxed or freezer
paper mix meal or flour with salt and pepper and spread the mixture over the paper. Dip the tomato slices into the egg and lay
out on the flour mixture, turning to coat all sides. Heat 2 tablespoons olive oil and 2 tablespoons unsalted butter to cover the
bottom of a sauté pan over medium heat. Tap excess flour off the
tomato slices and place in the hot fat. Fry until golden brown on
both sides and the wall of the tomato is fork-tender. Sprinkle with
salt to taste and a grinding of pepper. Keep the heat low enough
so that the vegetables turn golden brown while cooking through
and add more oil and butter as needed. If excess flour builds up
in the oil and blackens, wipe the pan clean with a paper towel,
add more oil and butter, and continue.

Salsas and Sauces

Green Tomato Raita

*W*E knew immediately that green tomatoes were naturals for these little sweet and sour or hot and mild salad sauces — so cool, so refreshing. This first one is a cooling Indian relish with yogurt, one of the most effective cures for the hot-mouth syndrome caused by too many hot peppers. Delicious and refreshing alone or to serve with hot dishes, such as Chicken with Green Tomato Curry (p. 36), or over fish or as a salad dressing. Try it as a sauce for cucumbers.

Makes 2½ cups

1 cup plain low-fat yogurt
1 cup chopped green tomatoes
½ cup chopped scallions
2 tablespoons finely chopped cilantro

1 tablespoon minced fresh green chiles
1 teaspoon cumin seeds, roasted
1 teaspoon minced ginger
½ teaspoon salt

Stir all ingredients together and set aside at room temperature for 1 hour to let the flavors blend.

Roasted Green Tomato Salsa

We knew all along we wanted to infuse a green tomato with a roasted flavor, to accompany meats, fowl, or fish. The roasted flavor comes from the tomatoes and the cumin seeds, both of which are subjected to fire, while honey smoothes all the disparate elements into one entity. It was wonderful served with a charcoal-grilled halibut steak one night. When fruit juice was substituted for the honey, it complemented the Hickory Grilled Pork Loin (p. 140). It should be made several hours before serving. Grilling can be done over an outdoor grill or in a ridged pan on the range.

Makes about 2 cups

2 medium green tomatoes (12 ounces), sliced thin

½ meaty red bell pepper, grilled, skinned, and slivered

1 tablespoon cumin seeds, roasted

½ Granny Smith apple, chopped fine

2 garlic cloves, smashed, skinned, and minced

½ jalapeño pepper (or more), seeded and minced

½ cup chopped cilantro leaves

1 teaspoon salt and a grind of pepper or to taste

2 tablespoons good, green, virgin olive oil

2 tablespoons lime juice

1 teaspoon honey or 2 tablespoons orange juice concentrate if serving with pork

1 bunch of arugula leaves

Grill the tomatoes over a quick fire so that the slices blacken and sizzle but do not become soft. Cut in half-inch dice and toss in a bowl with the sweet pepper, crushed cumin, apple, garlic, jalapeño, and cilantro. Add the salt and pepper, olive oil, lime juice, and the honey or orange juice concentrate, toss, and taste for seasonings. Cover and refrigerate, preferably overnight. Taste again for seasonings before serving on a bed of arugula.

Lemony Green Sauce for Pasta

Serve this silky, rich sauce over spiral pasta in small portions as a first course in the Italian manner, or to accompany a grilled meat.

Serves 4

½ **pound dried rotini or fusilli**	**grated zest of 1 large lemon**
3 tablespoons butter	½ **teaspoon salt**
1 teaspoon minced garlic	⅔ **cup Crème Fraîche (p. 56)**
2 large green tomatoes (1 pound), peeled, seeded, and chopped	**freshly ground pepper**

Bring a large pot of salted water to the boil in which to prepare the pasta as you make the sauce. Melt the butter in a skillet over medium heat, then add the garlic, green tomatoes, zest, and salt, and stew together for about 5 minutes. Stir in the Crème Fraîche, turn up the heat a bit to bring to a boil, and reduce until slightly thickened, stirring occasionally. Add pepper and spoon over the hot, drained pasta.

Two Greenly Refreshing Soups

Green Gazpacho with Almonds

WE had not heard of soups made with green tomatoes. Of course, we had not heard of many things made with green tomatoes, but on a hot day we seized on Eugene Walter's simple idea of a chicken broth flavored with lemon peel, celery seed, and dill, with coarsely chopped green tomatoes simmered in it. It could be pureed, and a spoonful of Crème Fraîche floated on top. From there the following green gazpacho, as well as the Buttermilk Shrimp Soup (p. 32), seemed made for the tang of green tomatoes.

Fresh and tart on a hot day, this soup with its touch of tarragon is wonderful. We've used hazelnuts instead of almonds with great success. It is best the longer it chills in its own juices.

Croutons

Be sure not to start snacking on these or you won't have any left for the salad or soup. The garlic can be omitted, as can the salt, and/or chopped herbs added toward the end. They can be made any size and cooked very slowly — for as long as 2 hours — so that they thoroughly dry. We find they're best if they're salted while browning. They can be used immediately, stored for a few days in a plastic bag, or frozen.

Makes 4 cups

½ loaf good-quality, chewy
    country-style bread
⅓ to ½ cup olive oil — not your
    best, but not your worst
2 garlic cloves, smashed, peeled,
    and chopped
2 teaspoons coarse salt

The bread should be a little stale or else it will absorb too much oil for our own good. In any case, slice it into ½-inch cubes — about 4 cups. Put the cubes in a large colander or spread on a cookie sheet to let them dry for several hours.

Heat a large sauté pan over medium heat. Put the bread cubes and the garlic into a large earthenware bowl and toss with the smaller amount of oil, adding more if needed to coat the cubes lightly. Pour into the hot pan, turn the heat to low, sprinkle with salt, and intermittently toss and shake the cubes until brown and crisp all over. Over a very low heat this could take an hour or more.

Serves 4 to 6

2 large green tomatoes (1 pound), cored and chunked
1 large, meaty green pepper, seeded and chunked
1 cucumber, peeled and cut in chunks
1 garlic clove, peeled
1 teaspoon salt
¼ cup tarragon vinegar

1½ teaspoons fresh tarragon or
½ teaspoon dried
2 cups chicken broth (if canned, delete salt)
freshly ground pepper to taste
½ cup blanched almonds
2 tablespoons olive oil
extra-virgin olive oil
Croutons

Place green tomatoes, green pepper, cucumber, garlic clove, salt, vinegar, and tarragon in a food-processor bowl in two batches and puree. Place in a bowl and stir in the broth and pepper. Chill at least 1 hour. Correct seasonings. Sauté the almonds in 2 tablespoons oil until golden brown, cool, puree in the food processor, and stir into the soup. To serve, ladle the soup into cups, drizzle a teaspoon of oil into each cup, and top with Croutons.

Buttermilk Shrimp Soup

Scrumptious, cooling, and refreshing in the summer heat, with a bit of bite. Add more buttermilk if any is left the next day, as we find the flavor and texture fade. For from-scratch fish broth you may substitute 1 fish bouillon cube (Knorr's makes a good one) dissolved in 2 cups of water, or use 1½ cups bottled clam broth with ½ cup water.

Serves 4

2 cups fish broth
½ pound medium to
   large shrimp
2 large green tomatoes
   (1 pound)
2 scallions, minced
2 jalapeño peppers (or
   more to taste), seeded
   and minced

1 tablespoon minced
   cilantro
1 teaspoon salt
¼ teaspoon freshly
   ground pepper
2 cups buttermilk

Bring broth to a boil in a small pot over medium-high heat. Add the shrimp and cook 1 minute, until they curl and turn pink. Drain, reserving the liquid. Cool shrimp in cold water, then drain, peel, and chop coarsely. Char the tomatoes over a flame, turning quickly just to char all sides for a roasted flavor. They should still be firm. Core, quarter, and finely chop them in the bowl of a food processor. Strain the reserved shrimp broth through a coffee filter, paper towel, or cheesecloth into a bowl. Stir in the tomatoes, shrimp, scallions, jalapeños, cilantro, salt, pepper, and buttermilk. Chill for several hours. Correct seasonings and serve.

Green Vegetable Dishes

Grilled Pale Vegetable Casserole

*T*HIS was invented for a community cookout years ago through necessity. There was nothing really "ripe," so I combined a mess of baby vegetables and leaves with green tomatoes in an aluminum foil packet to put on the grill. Since then, I've made it out of every combination of pale vegetable imaginable, starting always with green tomatoes and almost always including new potatoes, and it is always greeted enthusiastically, perhaps because many of the vegetables make their first appearance of the season in it, straight from garden to grill. Precise measurements are unnecessary for this dish.

Serves 6 to 8

3 tablespoons vegetable oil or butter

1½ quarts baby vegetables (such as turnips, okra, eggplant, green beans, cabbage, leeks, onions, zucchini or summer squash, spinach leaves, chard, garlic cloves, peas, immature garlic bulbs, fava beans)

2 cups new baby potatoes

2 large green tomatoes (1 pound), cored and cut in sixths

leaves of herbs, such as basil, sage, chervil, or thyme

oil or butter to top

salt and pepper

Crisscross two large sheets of heavy-duty aluminum foil in a pan or bowl for structure. Coat the bottom with vegetable oil or butter. Clean the vegetables well and pare into attractive shapes, leaving tiny ones whole. Place the harder vegetables in the bottom of the packet and the juicier ones on top. Top with the green tomato sections, scatter with herbs, drizzle with oil and/or butter, and sprinkle with ample salt and pepper to taste. Bring the foil edges together in a careful seam, for you will put this package over a medium-hot grill and turn it several times to make sure that the hard vegetables are done on all sides. Approximate grilling time is 35 minutes.

Test for doneness by turning the packet seam side up and open it a bit to fork-test the vegetables. If they need more cooking time, pinch the foil back together, but if they are tender, spoon straight from the foil as from a casserole.

Green Tomato Quiche

The richness of the custard, crust, and bacon is offset by the tartness of green tomato and mellowness of the leeks. Serve in small, warm wedges.

Serves 8 to 10

1 recipe Italian Butter
　　Pastry
4 ounces or 3 thick-cut
　　slices of bacon, cut
　　into ¼-inch strips
2 cups coarsely chopped
　　leeks, washed well
　　(5 ounces)
1 teaspoon fresh thyme
　　leaves

1 teaspoon salt
8 ounces green tomatoes
　　(1 large or 2
　　medium), sliced
　　thinly
pepper to taste
1 large egg plus 1 yolk
¾ cup heavy cream
1 cup shredded Gruyère
　　cheese (3 ounces)

Italian Butter Pastry

**Makes enough pastry for one
10-inch or two 8-inch or 9-
inch one-crust tarts**

**1¾ cups unbleached flour
1 tablespoon sugar
½ teaspoon salt
10 tablespoons unsalted butter
⅓ cup very cold water**

*A food processor makes this
best. Put the flour, sugar, and salt
in the bowl with the metal blade
and whir to blend. Add the
chilled butter and pulse until the
mixture resembles cornmeal. Pour
the water into the bowl. Whir just
until the dough begins to come together. Put on a piece of waxed
paper or plastic wrap and bring
together into a ball. Wrap and
chill for at least 1 hour.*

Preheat the oven to 400 degrees. Roll the crust and fit it into
a 10-inch removable-bottom tart pan. Line with foil and weight
with dried beans or rice. Bake about 7 minutes, until set. Remove foil carefully, prick the crust with a fork, and bake another
10 minutes, until bottom is lightly browned. Let it cool while you
make the filling. Reduce oven heat to 350 degrees.

Render the bacon pieces over medium heat until almost crisp,
remove from the pan, and drain on a paper towel. Pour all but
1 tablespoon fat out of the pan, add the leeks, thyme, ½ teaspoon
salt, and the bacon. Cover and cook over low heat about 5 minutes. Add the tomatoes and a few grinds of pepper, cover the pan,
and allow the mixture to sweat over low heat for 5 minutes. Uncover and let it cool.

Lightly beat the egg and yolk together with the cream and remaining ½ teaspoon salt. Sprinkle half the cheese over the pastry, add the vegetables, and pour the custard mixture over. Top
with the remaining cheese and bake 25 to 30 minutes or until
custard is set. Cool 5 minutes before serving.

Early Main Dishes

Chicken with Green Tomato Curry

*L*UNCH or supper dishes to eat outside on the picnic table or by a stone wall with bees humming sexily in the throats of the foxgloves. At this time of year, you'll find you simply can't stay inside.

Slightly hot to the tongue, intensely but delicately curry flavored, and colorful, this should be served with the perfumed rice, basmati. The intriguing texture and taste of this dish are complemented by the Green Tomato Raita (p. 27) and/or the Fresh Red and Green Indian Chutney (p. 41). Coconut milk is available canned, usually in the gourmet section of the grocery store. A new, "lite," low-fat version has just been introduced, for those who want to avoid saturated fat.

Serves 6

2 tablespoons vegetable oil

6 chicken thigh and leg quarters, skin removed

1½ cups coarsely chopped green tomatoes

1-inch knob of fresh gingerroot

2 garlic cloves, smashed and peeled

1 medium onion, peeled and quartered

½ cup unsweetened coconut milk (freeze the rest)

1 tablespoon hot curry powder

1 teaspoon salt

Heat oil in a large skillet and brown the chicken on both sides over medium-high heat. Place remaining ingredients in the bowl of a food processor and pulse to mince solid ingredients. Add to pan with chicken and bring to a simmer. Cover, lower heat, and cook 25 minutes or until the chicken is tender.

Shrimp and Scallop Fritters with Salsa Verde

This cool green sauce can be served with grilled or poached fish, or in the Italian way with cold sliced meats such as flank steak, as well as with the scallop fritters. Plump pillows of curly parsley are beautiful grown in the garden, but there is no comparison with the flavor of the flat-leaf Italian. Grow them both if you can.

Makes 2 cups sauce; the fritters serve 4

For the Salsa Verde:

2 medium green tomatoes, cored and quartered (about ⅔ pound)	1 shallot, peeled
	¼ teaspoon salt
	¼ teaspoon freshly ground pepper
3 tablespoons minced fresh Italian parsley	3 tablespoons white wine tarragon vinegar
1½ tablespoons minced fresh tarragon	3 tablespoons extra-virgin olive oil
1½ tablespoons capers, rinsed and drained	

Place all the ingredients in the bowl of a food processor and process 30 seconds or until the ingredients are finely chopped but not pureed. Serve at room temperature.

Variation: Add 4 anchovy fillets, rinsed, dried, and chopped.

37

For the Shrimp and Scallop Fritters:

½ pound sea scallops
1 egg white
1 shallot, peeled
½ teaspoon salt
⅛ teaspoon ground white
   pepper
pinch of cayenne

⅓ cup heavy cream or
   Crème Fraîche
   (p. 56)
½ pound large shrimp,
   peeled and diced
1 cup dry Bread Crumbs
   (p. 90)
vegetable oil for frying

Place scallops, egg white, shallot, salt, pepper, and cayenne in the bowl of a food processor and puree until smooth, about 30 seconds. Add cream and pulse several times until cream is blended in. Scrape into a bowl and stir the shrimp into the mixture. Place the crumbs on waxed paper and, using 2 tablespoons of the shrimp mixture for each fritter, drop onto the crumbs and gently coat. Place cakes on a waxed-paper–lined cookie sheet and chill for at least 1 hour. Heat ¼ inch of oil in a skillet over medium heat until it shimmers. Add 3 or 4 fritters (do not crowd) and cook 2 to 3 minutes per side, until golden brown, then remove fritters with a slotted spoon and place them on a brown paper bag, which will absorb any excess oil. Repeat with the remaining fritter mixture. Serve immediately with the room-temperature Salsa Verde.

Transitional Salads — Green and Red Together

Soft Green Tomato Salad with Pumpkin-Seed Dressing

$\mathcal{M}$ADELEINE Kamman, like so many European and old-style cooks, calls for green tomatoes for salads — not hard green tomatoes, but yellow or pink, those with some juice, which have been allowed to develop some flavor on the vine, but which are an entirely different vegetable from red, ripe tomatoes. For them she calls for a dressing of orange and lemon juices, grated rinds and chives, as well as oil, salt, and pepper. In another salad, she lays the unripe tomato slices down on a bed of Italian parsley and pale green celery leaves, interspersing them with a Gruyère or fontina cheese. The dressing is made with saffron threads and fennel vinegar as well as basil leaves. Patience Gray advises the same in one of my favorite books, *Honey from a Weed,* but says that Greek and Catalonian salad tomatoes seem to be larger and firmer, with a fruity taste — crisp, perfumed, and sweet. They would be cut in half, stuffed with slices of peeled garlic, sprinkled with salt and oregano or wild marjoram, topped with very thinly sliced sweet white onion, perhaps an anchovy, and when eaten would have fruity olive oil poured over them.

Use firm, first-ripe tomatoes for this salad.

39

Makes 1 cup of dressing

3 tablespoons olive oil	2 tablespoons fruity
1 cup pumpkin seeds	olive oil
1 teaspoon salt	1 tablespoon lemon
½ teaspoon cumin seeds	juice
¼ teaspoon freshly	tomatoes
ground pepper	greens

Heat a medium-sized sauté pan over medium heat. When it is hot, add the olive oil, and when that is wavy hot pour in the pumpkin seeds (save a few for garnish) and toss until coated with oil. Sprinkle with salt and toss. Turn the heat to medium low and cook, stirring often, until the pumpkin seeds are brown. If the heat is too high, the seeds will pop like corn, which is fine if you are careful not to let them burn. When they are crisp and brown, set them aside to cool.

In a small, heavy-bottomed pan over low heat roast the cumin seeds until they give off their aroma, then put them in a mortar. When they are cool, pound them until powdered, then add the pumpkin seeds ¼ cup by ¼ cup by ¼ cup (reserving a few of these roasted ones for garnish) and grind them. When they form a paste, add the pepper, olive oil, and lemon juice, and then add salt to taste.

Alternatively, you can grind the seeds in a spice or coffee grinder (see p. 14), and then put them in a bowl to mix with the oil and juice.

Drizzle over slices of pale green/pink tomato on a bed of buttery greens such as arugula or Boston lettuce or watercress. Garnish with a mixture of the raw and roasted whole pumpkin seeds.

Fresh Red and Green Indian Chutney

We find ourselves folding this easily made condiment into yogurt for a low-fat lunch, but it is meant to be served as an accompaniment to Indian meals, as a salsa with toasted pita chips, or on a sandwich as described on p. 67. Try it as a dressing to perk up salad greens.

Makes 2½ cups

½ pound green tomatoes
   (2 medium)
½ pound ripe tomatoes
   (2 medium)
1-inch knob of
   gingerroot, peeled
   and coarsely chopped
1 large garlic clove,
   peeled

6 sprigs of fresh cilantro
¾ teaspoon salt
¼ teaspoon ground
   cumin
¼ teaspoon crushed red
   pepper flakes

Place all ingredients in the bowl of a food processor and pulse on and off so that the mixture does not puree but is finely chopped. Let it sit at least an hour before serving to allow flavors to mellow.

Warm Zucchini Salad

A *New York Times* article on Italian women restaurant chefs contained the impetus for this recipe of zucchini, red and green tomatoes, pine nuts, and basil, all sautéed very briefly in the most fragrant olive oil. The final perfumed taste hints of much more than its simple parts. To use as a small colorful garnish, dice the ingredients finely and uniformly.

Serves 4 to 6

2 tablespoons olive oil
¾ pound zucchini, thinly sliced, about 3 cups
1 large red tomato, peeled, seeded, and chopped (1 cup)
1 large green tomato, peeled, seeded, and chopped (1 cup)

freshly ground pepper
2 tablespoons white wine vinegar
¼ cup toasted pine nuts
1 tablespoon minced fresh basil
¼ teaspoon salt

Heat the olive oil in a large skillet and toss the zucchini slices over medium-high heat for about 3 to 5 minutes, until they begin to wilt. Add tomatoes and pepper and toss together for 2 minutes. Turn heat to high and sprinkle on the vinegar. Toss vegetables to coat and let any liquid evaporate. This takes only about a minute. Stir in pine nuts, basil, and salt. Remove from heat, cool to lukewarm, and serve.

Condiments

Old-Fashioned Pickle Parcels

ALTHOUGH green tomatoes make the ultimate pickle, and pickling is an ancient method of preserving food, it is interesting to see from early cookery books other ways. One method calls for laying down slices of green tomatoes between layers of salt in a cask. The same was done with cucumbers, artichokes, lima and string beans, and nasturtiums. The cask was filled with alternating layers of salt and vegetables, a board was placed on top, and the salt was moistened occasionally. More vegetables could be added day by day. To prevent the brine from sliming, one was advised to place a thick layer of horseradish tops over the top! To use the vegetables, they were soaked in cold water overnight and cooked twice, in a change of water. Many preferred this way of preserving to canning.

We were fascinated by our mind's-eye picture of these Pickle Parcels when we read the original receipt by Mrs. Sarah T. Rorer, who was a "principal of the Philadelphia Cooking School," and whose book, *How to Cook Vegetables,* was published by the vegetable people themselves, W. Atlee Burpee & Co. of Philadelphia, in 1903. These are cunning little packages of hollowed-out green tomatoes stuffed with a sweet and sour cabbage mixture, then recapped and the resulting package tied with twine and pickled. They are scrumptious. We make them slightly sweet and use them to accompany roasts or quiche alike, or as a snack. The recipe can be doubled — the original one called for 2 heads of cabbage, which I believe would have been used to stuff at least 24 tomatoes. Of course, we use only the very freshest ingredients, straight from the garden or farmers' market.

6 smooth, soft green tomatoes; a little pink does not hurt, and may make the finished dish sweeter
¼ cup coarse salt, approximately
½ head of cabbage
1 tablespoon whole mustard seeds
¼ teaspoon ground cloves

¼ teaspoon ground allspice
soft white cotton twine for tying
6 cups cold white vinegar
3 chipotles or other dried hot peppers
3 garlic cloves, peeled

From the stem end of each tomato slice a piece large enough to allow the removal of the seeds without breaking the tomato and reserve. With a melon baller or a grapefruit knife, take out the seeds and the ribs, but do not damage the outer wall. Sprinkle the inside of each tomato with 1 teaspoon of salt and set them upright in a glass, plastic, or crockery container large enough to hold the tomatoes in one layer, with each one's top next to it. Cover with cold water and soak for 24 hours. Next day, take the tomatoes from the water and drain upside down.

While they're draining, shred the cabbage into a large crockery bowl, toss with the remainder of the salt, and set it aside for half an hour until it begins to give off its moisture. Cover with cold water, swish to remove the salt, and drain in a colander. Rinse and dry the bowl, then take double handfuls of the cabbage from the colander, squeeze out the liquid, and replace the cabbage in the bowl. It will still be quite salty. Toss with the mustard, cloves, and allspice and pack gently into the tomatoes. Replace each top, packing the cabbage in, and tie them snugly with the soft twine.

Scald the container in which you salted the tomatoes, along with a plate of a size to fit inside it. Place the tomatoes upright in it, cover with the cold vinegar, add the peppers and the garlic, place the scalded plate over the top of the tomatoes, place a sheet of plastic over the plate and up over the edges of the container so as to seal out any contaminants, and weight the plastic-covered plate with a clean brick, a large can of tomatoes placed in a plastic bag, or a container of water sufficiently heavy to hold the plate under the vinegar. Careful it's not so heavy it crushes the tomatoes. Let sit in a cool place for at least a week, then serve.

Grandma Bertha's Green Tomato Crock Pickles

Many of the methods that Andy Snyder and Chris Anderson follow for their popular Fire Hill Farm preserves came from Andy's grandma Bertha, who brought them from Russia when she came here alone at the age of fifteen. "Her porch in Connecticut was covered with barrels — pickled herring, pickled tomatoes, and sauerkraut — and she would say, 'I will teach you my recipes if you will make them for me when I get to be an old lady and can no longer do them for myself,'" Andy told me. He made them for her each year until she died. Now Chris and Andy make them to sell at the Rutland County Farmers' Market and at their own farm stand, as well as by mail order.

For this recipe, the herbs and seasonings are divided, half to go on the bottom of the crock and half on top of the tomatoes. These pickles are naturally fermented, in the manner of good sauerkraut: "You don't need vinegar if you make a good pickle." And Andy wouldn't use anything but his own fresh, organic tomatoes. He makes these pickles mid-season, from the small, early tomatoes and again at the end of the season with the last green tomatoes "that would see frost before red." Don't disturb these while they're fermenting.

Andy makes them in plastic 5-gallon pails and keeps them in a cool, draft-free cellar, well into the following spring, canning only those he will sell at his stand. Use a 5-gallon crock if you have it.

4 gallons small to medium-sized green tomatoes, freshly picked

6 very full stalks of dill

8 garlic cloves, peeled and cut into thirds

6 tablespoons mixed pickling spice

4 tablespoons mustard seeds

15 bay leaves

4 teaspoons crushed hot pepper

9 quarts good water (no chlorine, please)

1½ cups coarse canning salt

Rinse tomatoes in cool water and let drain dry. Clean and sterilize a 5-gallon crock or other container and a plate that will fit inside of it with boiling water. Strew half of the dill, garlic, pickling spice, mustard seeds, bay leaves, and hot pepper on the bottom of the crock. Add tomatoes until the container is ⅞ full, then strew the remaining spices over the top of the tomatoes. Place the plate over the tomatoes.

Make a brine by bringing 2 quarts of the water to a boil, then stir in the salt until it is fully dissolved. Add the remaining 7 quarts of cold water, mix thoroughly, and pour the warm solution over the tomatoes until the tomatoes and plate are fully submerged. Cover tomatoes and plate with a large piece of plastic that can keep contaminants out. Weight the plate with clean bricks or heavy cans of food, first putting the weight in a plastic bag to guard against corrosion.

Keep the crock in a draft-free location at 60 to 65 degrees for at least two weeks before you peek inside. At that point the tomatoes may have started to ferment. Skim any risen yeast off the top with a slotted spoon (a paddle-shaped cream skimmer works great here) and allow the tomatoes to continue to work for another two weeks before tasting.

You may keep them in the container in a cold cellar almost indefinitely, if you started with good fresh tomatoes and treated them correctly. However, you may feel you should can them.

If so, take the tomatoes from the crock, cut them in halves or quarters, and pack them tightly in pint or quart canning jars, leaving ¼ inch of headroom. Strain the brine into a pan and heat to a boil. Pour over the tomatoes and bubble the brine by sliding a thin knife or spatula around the perimeter of each jar. Top off the brine, leaving ¼ inch of headroom. Cap the jars and submit to a boiling water bath, 15 minutes for pints, 20 minutes for quarts.

Part 2

That First Ripe Tomato,
Straight from the Vine

THAT FIRST RIPE TOMATO? Eat it right in the garden, while it's plumply sun-hot and the green scent of tomato vine curls to your nose. But first you must heed the advice of our artist friend — feel it first, heft it in the curve of your palm, and only then eat it. In the evening, slice the second fatly onto a pretty plate. Perhaps you'll serve the slices plain or with the merest sprinkling of salt and sugar. But if you are unable to resist popping out the kitchen door to pluck a sprig of spicy basil to tear roughly over them, perhaps to be followed by a bit of chopped garlic, a drizzle of peppery green olive oil, then your instincts are good, for if these are embellishments they are ones born in food heaven. In a few days you'll go even further, strewing a mixture of bread crumbs and grated Parmesan on top of the garlic and running the dish under the broiler until the top is browned and the tomatoes are just beginning to give out their juice. *That* will be fine.

That will be something you'll remember in February, for in spite of the fact that we complain, we northerners, about the rarity of finding a good tomato when this growing season is over, a few of us think the fact that modern growing and shipping methods have not yet found a way to make good tomatoes available all year round is satisfactory in its own right. For now, good tomatoes remain a food of the season, and during that season they make an imperative — enjoy them to the utmost! It's feast or famine, so now let's enjoy the feast.

Sliced Tomatoes, Cold and Hot

Sliced Tomatoes with Various Toppings

*I*N older days, tomatoes were listed in menus in the back of cookery books the likes of Mrs. Rorer's. They are therein called for being baked, broiled, and sauced, but most often simply sliced, for breakfast as well as for lunch and dinner, and for suppers besides.

Plain sliced tomatoes are just fine, and certainly a plateful of them appeared almost every evening on our childhood supper table. (Ed Behr notes, however, that most of the aroma/taste of a tomato disappears within minutes of slicing, so don't let them sit.) Following my father's example, we even sprinkled sugar over them. My daughter takes sugar on tomatoes as much for granted as I do. Her summer camp lunch always includes cherry tomatoes with a packet of sugar to dip them in.

Michigan readers of the *Detroit Free Press*'s exposé of my sugar and tomato habit were overwhelmingly sympathetic to that midwestern predilection, and I've found since that to Italian and French cooks a pinch of sugar, particularly in conjunction with salt, brings out the flavor and is an accepted way to treat a slice of tomato around the world. In fact, treating tomatoes as a tart fruit, with sweetening, is not uncommon, as witness the Sweet Tomato Gratin with Crème Fraîche in this section, and in other desserts.

Of course, given heatproof plates, any of the suggestions for sliced tomatoes with their good toppings could be run under a broiler until it is bubbling quite nicely. And that would be a form of gratin, although that term more properly calls up the vision of a crusty topping of cheese and/or bread crumbs.

So, when familiarity sanctions the view that it is perfectly all right to paint the lily, do allow the following toppings to incite your imagination, and don't forget to exploit to the utmost the fantasia of textures, colors, and sizes as well as summer scents to be found in your garden and your farmers' market. White crockery plates provide the perfect frame for spicy purple basil sprinkled over slices of yellow tomatoes resting on a few leaves of curly greens, perhaps punctuated with shards of chocolate pepper. Toss squares of fragrant roasted yellow peppers with red cherry tomatoes and nuggets of white mozzarella in a leafy cup of white and red radicchio. Ah, summer!

Over a plate of sliced tomatoes:

• crumble soft bleu or Gorgonzola cheese, then whisk together some wine vinegar, salt, pepper, and fruity olive oil and drizzle over all;

• grate some Asiago cheese, scatter some fresh torn basil, and sprinkle with a tablespoon of pine nuts toasted with olive oil and minced garlic;

• which have been interspersed with slices of the best fresh mozzarella you can find, toss whole basil leaves and drizzle with a bit of fruity olive oil;

• spread olive paste, or chopped oil-cured olives, and sprinkle first with a good red wine vinegar and then with minced Italian flat-leaf parsley;

• dollop a mixture of half whipped cream/half mayonnaise into which finely chopped red onion has been folded. Call it "Tomatoes Chantilly"; or replace the red onions with a tablespoon or two of good quality horseradish, which has been drained. Grind black pepper coarsely over all;

• sprinkle salt and pepper, then pour over them Crème Fraîche (p. 56) or a good heavy sweet cream into which has been stirred an extravagant amount of your favorite herb, minced. Be adventurous, now — how about mint? Low-calorie? Use yogurt instead. Or leave small tomatoes whole, core and peel them, scatter torn herbs over, pour the heavy cream over, dust with salt and pepper, and serve;

• trail spoonfuls of our Green Tomato Raita (p. 27);

• which have been alternated with avocado slices, pour over a dressing that you have whisked together of lime juice, salt, scallions, and olive oil;

• crumble crisp bacon. Whisk up our Tomato Vinaigrette (p. 97) and drizzle over all;

• spread herbed goat cheese (thinned, if needed, with a bit of olive oil) and drizzle with our Red Pepper Oil (p. 73);

• sprinkle toasted walnuts and a garlicky, lemony dressing made with either mayonnaise or olive oil;

• into which leaves of lovage or celery have been tucked, along with slices of cucumber, spoon a small salad of very thinly sliced fennel and celery, which has been marinated at least a few hours in white wine vinegar, crushed garlic, and olive oil;

• interspersed with slices of hard-boiled egg, sprinkle with chopped shallots, garlic, salt, balsamic vinegar, coarsely ground pepper, then decorate with shavings of Parmesan cheese and a sprinkling of good olive oil;

• drizzle a dressing of pounded parsley, salt, garlic, and olive oil;

• tucked with the leaves and flowers of nasturtiums, pour over a dressing of mustard and cream with salt and pepper that you've whisked up, and sieve hard-boiled egg yolks over all.

Marilyn's Country-Baked Tomatoes

We were used to slicing tomatoes thickly, or only in halves, placing them in a single layer in an oiled baking dish, and scattering them with torn basil leaves, chopped garlic, bread crumbs, and then grated Parmesan cheese. We drizzled the whole sparingly with olive oil, sprinkled it with salt and pepper, and ran the dish under the broiler until the top was browned. The tomatoes were merely warmly wilted in contrast to the hot and crusty topping.

After the first edition of *T.I.!* came out, Marilyn Thomas, a friend from Dowagiac, Michigan, wrote to say she'd gotten this recipe from a 1912 cookbook. She calls it "old-fashioned fast food with a really *good* flavor in fresh tomato season." Similar recipes appear in early cookery books, including Mrs. Rorer's. We find that good fresh whole-wheat crumbs add a sweetness that is welcome. The crumbs can be toasted if you prefer. It just goes to show there is nothing new under the sun, only things we don't know about yet.

Serves 4

4 tablespoons unsalted butter	3 large tomatoes, thinly sliced (1½ pounds)
1½ cups fresh whole-wheat Bread Crumbs (p. 90)	coarse salt freshly ground pepper

Preheat oven to 350 degrees. Use a bit of the butter to prepare a small gratin pan or a 9-inch glass pie plate. Alternately layer crumbs and tomatoes, sprinkle with salt and pepper, and dot with butter. The top layer should be crumbs, seasoned and dotted with butter. Bake for 1 hour or until golden brown. Serve warm or cold.

Red and Yellow Gratin for a Hot Day

An exquisite gratin redolent of the scents and juices of Provençal France is described by many cookery writers, perhaps most notably by Mireille Johnston in her excellent *Cuisine of the Sun*, who names it for its color — Tian Rouge. It is a brilliantly colored dish of roasted red peppers and tomatoes, with Provençal herbs of parsley and basil and thyme, dusted with bread crumbs and baked in a hot oven, then served cold in a sun-dappled shady place on a hot and sunny day. We pay homage to that great dish as we offer you our version. Remember to make it early enough to let it come to room temperature before serving.

Serves 6

5 tablespoons extra-virgin olive oil

2 large ripe red tomatoes and 2 large ripe yellow tomatoes, thickly sliced (2 pounds altogether)

1 red and 1 yellow pepper, both large and meaty, roasted, skinned, and cut into ¼-inch strips

6 anchovy fillets, cleaned and cut in little pieces

16 oil-cured black olives, pitted and chopped

2 teaspoons minced garlic

2 tablespoons minced Italian parsley

salt

freshly ground pepper

Heat oven to 350 degrees. Spread 1 tablespoon of the oil in a 1½-quart shallow gratin or baking dish. Overlap tomato slices, alternating colors. Sprinkle lightly with salt and pepper, dot with half the anchovies, olives, garlic, and parsley, and drizzle with 2 tablespoons of olive oil. Spread the roasted pepper strips over this and dot with remaining anchovies, garlic, olives, and parsley. Sprinkle lightly again with salt and pepper and drizzle remaining olive oil over all. Bake 1 hour. Cool and serve warm or at room temperature with crusty bread to sop up the delectable juices.

Sweet Tomato Gratin with Crème Fraîche

A very old, quite classic technique more than recipe. Jasper White treats wild berries in this manner and details it in *Jasper White's Cooking from New England*, which is a mainstay on our shelves, but we've found it a number of times in old recipe books done to tomatoes, using sour cream. It can be prepared with as few as two nicely ripe and flavorful tomatoes, or with as many as you like. You may substitute sour cream for the Crème Fraîche.

Serves 6

6 fat, ripe, juicy red tomatoes, sliced thick
2 cups very thick Crème Fraîche

grated zest of 1 lemon
½ cup brown sugar

Let tomato slices drain on a rack for 15 minutes. Then preheat the broiler. Place the slices on an ovenproof plate or platter in a single layer. Spread thickly with the Crème Fraîche and sprinkle with the lemon zest and then the brown sugar. Run under the broiler until the sugar bubbles, becomes fragrant, and begins to caramelize. Watch it closely to prevent burning, remove, and serve as salad or dessert. It can also be served cold.

Crème Fraîche

It seems that this delectable, sweet and tart topping happens naturally in some airs; here it is made by whisking together equal amounts (usually 1 cup each) of sour cream and heavy sweet cream — the best quality you can find — in a small bowl until they are smoothly combined, then allowing them to sit in your kitchen until they become thickened and of the tang you like. This can take half an hour some days and all day on others. It may be whipped, although it is already thick; it may be sweetened with sugar, although it is not precisely sour. You can drizzle it on savory things — it is delicious on potatoes and turnips cooked and whipped together with milk and butter. Or it can replace whipped sweet or sour cream on almost any dessert.

Small Salads, Salsas, and Sauces

Espey's Basic Salsa

CALL them small salads, salsas, sauces, chutneys, little treats, small tastes, whatever, they all spell completion. Our small salads are nothing more — nor less — than a tomato, chopped, and put into a bowl with a little wine or balsamic vinegar and fruity olive oil. Slivers of onion, minced garlic, bits of hot pepper, torn leaves of spicy basil, potent cilantro, parsley, arugula, thyme, and/or mint, chunks of freshly pulled mozzarella, pitted and chopped black, oil-cured olives, fillets of anchovies washed of their salt, fat capers, thin curls of Parmesan pared off the loaf, bits of pineapple, fresh (and only fresh) peach — all are welcomed in their turn.

These salsas are then used on their own, to garnish a plate, to top luscious greens, to accompany fresh fish or roasts before or after cooking. They can begin to make soups, be added to broths along with bits of fish, meat with vegetables, or mushrooms reeking of the wild. They add verve to a plateful of plainly cooked beans, split peas, or lentils because their juicy piquancy complements the dry, earthy flavors of those foods. We crave them with scrambled or fried eggs or folded into an omelette. You may let a fragrant small salad of basil, olive oil, and tomatoes marinate all day, then release its flavorful fragrance by applying it to a hot starch. Or make delicious (and low-fat) sandwiches by mounding spoonfuls on good, fresh bread or Bruschetta (p. 90).

My picky ten-year-old spooned this or a variation onto Bruschetta and loved it. She still does, and so do I. Napkins, please — you tend to guzzle.

Makes 3 cups

2 large ripe tomatoes
   (1 pound)
1 medium white onion
1 large garlic clove
a handful of herbs of
   your choice: basil,
   cilantro, parsley,
   mint, sage, chopped
1 teaspoon salt

several grinds of pepper
2 tablespoons red wine
   vinegar
4 tablespoons fruity
   virgin olive oil
greens of your choice:
   arugula, radicchio,
   lettuce, cabbage

Core the tomatoes, halve, and gently squeeze out seeds. Chop coarsely and put into a small bowl. Halve the onion lengthwise and sliver. Add to the bowl. Smash, peel, and mince the garlic, and add to the bowl with the rest of the ingredients (except for the greens). Toss and set aside so that the flavors mingle. Serve on a bed of the greens.

Marinated Red Onion and Tomato Salad

A salad easy to prepare, with deep flavor. Take it on a picnic.

Serves 6

½ cup sliced red onion
4 large ripe tomatoes
   (2 pounds), cut in
   quarters or eighths
1 tablespoon brown
   sugar
¼ cup balsamic vinegar

½ teaspoon salt
freshly ground pepper
¼ cup good, fruity olive
   oil
1 tablespoon minced
   fresh basil

Toss all ingredients together in a large glass bowl, cover, and let marinate for several hours at room temperature, tossing every once in a while.

Tomato and Peach Salsa

The two fruits that, to our minds, are worth waiting for at their local and seasonal peak, are the tomato and the peach, and it is poetic justice to pair them. Besides being delicious with tortilla chips or as a side to grilled chicken or pork, this salsa is gorgeous. Make it at least an hour ahead of time to allow the flavors to pop out, and use the best ingredients, including balsamic vinegar, that you can find.

Makes 3 cups

1 large ripe peach
2 large ripe tomatoes
½ to 1 jalapeño pepper (to taste), minced
¼ large white onion, sliced lengthwise into shards (½ cup)
1 large garlic clove, smashed, peeled, and minced

3 tablespoons minced cilantro leaves
1 teaspoon salt or to taste
grind of pepper to taste
4 tablespoons balsamic vinegar

Plunge peach and tomatoes into boiling water until skins are loosened, about 10 seconds only. Drain and peel. Slice the peach to the pit around the equator, then thinly slice lengthwise off the pit into a bowl. Halve tomatoes and gently press out the seeds. Cut into bite-sized chunks and add to the peach slices. Add the minced jalapeño, onion shards, minced garlic, cilantro leaves, salt and pepper to taste, and stir in the vinegar. Taste for seasonings. Cover and set aside for at least an hour, then taste for seasonings again. You may want to add a bit more cilantro, although it should not be overpowering, or a bit more jalapeño.

Guacamole

The Aztecs ate guacamole made with tomatoes, capsicums (peppers), and avocados, as well as with the agave worm or maguey slug! For the worm, we substitute cilantro, which, along with the lime juice, is essential to give this guacamole its distinctive flavor. We grow cilantro profusely in season and then, because we can't count on quality out of season, process it with olive oil to freeze in small jars for winter use. Dip up this small salad with good flour or corn tortilla chips, dash it over greens, or layer it on Bruschetta (p. 90). Ruth does her chopping and mashing by hand so that it is very chunky, but I almost always do mine in a food processor.

Makes 3 cups

1 large garlic clove, smashed, peeled, and coarsely chopped
1 small hot pepper (or to taste)
1 small, sharp onion, peeled and coarsely chopped; or 6 scallions, with edible green included, coarsely chopped

¼ cup chopped cilantro leaves
1 large tomato (8 ounces), cored and chunked
2 ripe avocados
juice of 1 lime
salt to taste

Chop ingredients in order of appearance above, either with a cleaver on a board or by pulsing in the bowl of the food processor, so that the first four ingredients are chopped quite fine, the tomato adds small texture, and the avocados make their texture known. Then stir in the lime juice and salt to taste. Serve immediately, or make the surface airtight by applying plastic wrap directly to it, preventing the avocados from turning an unappetizing brown, and refrigerate until serving time.

Italian Bread and Tomato Salad

In her irreproachable *Celebrating Italy*, Carol Field describes a more traditional bread salad than this, wherein stale bread is moistened in water or a bit of broth, then mixed with fresh ripe tomatoes and fresh herbs, with the cruet of olive oil tipped over all and balsamic vinegar to flavor it. We've toasted our bread first, which can be any good sourdough or French bread, even whole grain, so long as it is not too dark and dense. If you have some of the olive oil flavored with the Stuffed Dried Tomatoes (p. 143) left over, use that to put the salad together.

Serves 4 to 6

6 1-inch-thick slices of good bread, cut from a baguette and cut into 1-inch cubes (or enough to equal 3 cups)

4 tablespoons olive oil

2 garlic cloves, smashed, peeled, and chopped

1 tablespoon coarse salt

2 large ripe tomatoes, cut into crescent eighths, the eighths halved

½ cup white onion, cut in shards

½ teaspoon salt

¼ teaspoon freshly ground pepper

1 teaspoon coarsely grained country mustard

3 tablespoons imported red wine vinegar

4 tablespoons olive oil

1 tablespoon walnut oil

2 medium heads of radicchio (or bitter greens such as escarole or chicory, or a combination), cored, cleaned, and torn

3 ounces Gruyère, shaved thin (or crumbled Gorgonzola)

3 tablespoons coarsely chopped, toasted walnuts

Make croutons with the bread cubes, olive oil, garlic, and salt, following the directions on pp. 30–31, toasting them over lowest heat until all the moisture is drawn out and they are very crisp. Let cool.

Meanwhile, place tomatoes and onion in a large bowl. In a small bowl whisk together the salt, pepper, mustard, and vinegar until the salt is dissolved. Whisk in the oils until well blended and pour over the tomatoes. Toss well and let sit for 1 hour at room temperature. Just before serving toss the dressed tomatoes and onion with the croutons, greens, cheese, and nuts.

Fresh Marinated Tomato Sauce with Pasta

This is a very simple sauce but it should never be taken for granted — if it took all the time and effort in the world it would be worth it. It is the essence of earthy freshness. Go out in the cool of the morning to find the freshest and most flavorful tomatoes and basil, make the sauce, and allow it to marinate all day in a cool place. We don't bother peeling the tomatoes, although some do, as the process cooks the tomatoes a little bit. Accompany the pasta and sauce with a salad of fresh mixed greens and herbs, including scallions and radishes, dressed simply, and serve with crusty bread.

Serves 6 hungry people

6 large field-fresh tomatoes	**1 medium white onion, sliced (optional)**
20 to 30 leaves of freshly picked basil	**¾ cup best green fruity olive oil**
2 garlic cloves, smashed and peeled	**coarse salt**
1 small hot pepper, chopped (optional)	**coarsely ground fresh pepper**
	1½ pounds spaghetti

Make the sauce in the morning and let it marinate all day. Core the tomatoes and cut them roughly into a crockery bowl. Tear the clean basil leaves over the tomatoes and throw in the garlic (along with the hot pepper and the onion if you are using them), then stir in the olive oil. Cover the bowl loosely and leave to marinate in a cool place.

Just before your guests sit down to dinner, cook the pasta according to package directions. Drain it very well. Remove the garlic from the marinating tomatoes, add salt and pepper to taste, pour the pasta into the bowl, and toss with the sauce. Take the pepper mill to the table along with the pasta.

Sautéed Fresh Tomato Sauce

"The art of cooking tomatoes lies mostly in cooking them enough. In whatever way prepared, they should be put on some hours before dinner." — Sarah Rutledge, *The Carolina Housewife* (1847)

There have always been many opinions as to the proper way to treat tomatoes, but it is a mystery as to why the belief arose that a tomato sauce had to be slow-cooked all day. It held sway until very recently and was probably just the hard-dying vestigial belief that tomatoes were poisonous.

We make this sauce with innumerable variations and at the drop of a hat. It's good as a basis for soup, as a sauce for meats or an omelette, or with pasta. We call for it in the Squash Stuffed with Lamb (p. 233). The recipe can be halved or doubled, oregano, sage, or thyme added, the cheese omitted. The flavor is enhanced by heating the oil before tossing the tomatoes into it; this gives the sauce a roasted, sweet flavor.

Makes 2 cups

¼ to ⅓ cup olive oil
4 large ripe tomatoes (2 pounds), peeled, seeded, and diced
4 garlic cloves, minced
1 small dried hot red pepper, minced

¼ cup red wine
½ teaspoon each salt and pepper or to taste
5 sprigs of parsley, minced
¼ cup grated Parmesan cheese

In a sauté pan heat the oil over medium heat. Add the tomatoes, garlic, and hot pepper all at once and stir. Add the wine, stir in the salt and pepper, turn burner to medium low, and simmer for 30 minutes. Just before serving, stir the parsley and cheese into the hot mixture.

Sandwiches

Sandwiches: The Grand List

FFW (Favorite Food Writer) Laurie Colwin liked to make the first sliced tomato into a sandwich by slathering the bread (our Tomato Pumpernickel Bread on p. 234 would be perfect) with mayonnaise, dusting it with celery salt, and layering on the thinly sliced tomatoes. She would eat it open-faced, or "with a lid."

Indeed, one of the best things you can do for yourself and a few of those first ripe tomatoes is to find a big, not-too-chewy piece of bread and a ripe tomato and treat them likewise. Tear a few leaves of basil over or sprinkle with a bit of sugar and salt and maybe some freshly ground pepper. Some people like to cover the tomato with bacon, add some crisp, unctuous greens like spinach or arugula or just plain lettuce, and some people like to grill the bread first, but really, it all comes down to the same thing — the absolutely peak tomato and the good bread.

Some of us think a grilled cheese sandwich is not complete unless it contains thinly sliced tomato that shrieks with heat by the time the cheese melts, to be eaten with shards of raw onion. Some of us remember those childhood noon sandwiches of white bread plumped with a mound of canned salmon mixed with mayonnaise and maybe some pickle relish (perhaps Leatha's French Pickle, p. 175), topped with thin slices of tomato. You had to eat quickly or the tomato would soak the bread, so this was not a school sandwich, but a back-porch-in-summer one, accompanied by a glass of cold milk.

Basic Mayonnaise

We keep eggs from neighbors' chickens at room temperature, but if you are at all concerned about eating raw eggs use a commercially prepared mayonnaise such as Hellman's. Whole eggs instead of just yolks make a lighter, less rich, but also less cloying finish.

Makes 2⅓ cups

2 large eggs, room temperature
½ teaspoon salt
2 cups olive oil
2 tablespoons lemon juice

Place eggs and salt in the bowl of a food processor and process 1 minute to blend. With machine running, very slowly pour in a steady thin stream of oil. Add lemon juice all at once and whir to blend.

Variations

Andalusian Mayonnaise

Stir 5 tablespoons of Dried Tomato Harissa (p. 144) into ¾ cup mayonnaise until smooth. Use in sandwiches, with grilled fish or lamburgers or grilled chicken breasts.

Spicy Tomato Mayonnaise

Mince 2 hot fresh chiles and fold in 1 cup peeled, seeded, and chopped tomatoes, ¾ cup mayonnaise, 2 tablespoons lime juice, 1 tablespoon chopped cilantro, and season with salt to taste.

Grilled Tuna with Andalusian Mayonnaise

Serves 4

Sprinkle 1½ pounds of fresh tuna that has been divided into 4 portions with 2 tablespoons of lemon juice and 4 tablespoons of olive oil. Let marinate for at least 20 minutes. Heat the grill. Sprinkle the fish with coarse salt and freshly ground or cracked pepper and grill according to the thickness of the fish — about 2½ minutes on each side of a ½-inch-thick fish. Serve spread with Andalusian Mayonnaise.

We think breads should almost always be warmed if they are not fresh from the oven. These are some other sandwich favorites:

- Havarti cheese over sliced tomatoes, on rye spread with dilled mustard, and then grilled;
- chèvre crumbled over sliced tomatoes strewn with chopped herbs (chives, oregano, thyme, basil, even dill), on split English muffins, all drizzled faintly with fruity olive oil and then broiled;
- slices of a caraway-flavored cheese such as Leyden (if available) or Tilsit, Westphalian ham, and tomatoes with a sprinkling of caraway on buttered Tomato Pumpernickel Bread (p. 234);
- grilled chicken spread with Dried Tomato Harissa (p. 144), wrapped in leaves of arugula, and tucked in a warm pita;
- sliced hard-boiled egg layered on both sides of a split baguette, lathered with Sautéed Fresh Tomato Sauce (p. 65), sprinkled with grated Swiss cheese, and broiled until brown;
- grilled tomatoes and yellow peppers layered on a warmed crusty roll spread lavishly with Mexican Pumpkin-Seed Dip (p. 93);
- a mixture of warm grilled eggplant, shredded fresh mozzarella, and tomato crescents in a whole-wheat pita;
- slices of smoked turkey with Fresh Red and Green Indian Chutney (p. 41) on French bread that has been buttered or drizzled with olive oil and lightly grilled;
- slices of Monterey Jack cheese over sliced tomatoes over Guacamole (p. 61) spread on corn tortillas, broiled just till cheese begins to melt;
- thinly sliced country ham on warm French bread spread with Tomato Hot Tarragon Jam (p. 151) mixed with horseradish and salt and pepper to taste;
- thin slices of good liverwurst topped with Leatha's French Pickle (p. 175) on buttered Tomato Pumpernickel Bread (p. 234);
- thin slices of tomato and rare roast beef on German pumpernickel spread with horseradish, sour cream, and mayonnaise;
- warm Mixed Vegetable Grill with Lamb (p. 136) on a hero roll or small, warmed baguette;

• thinking of a bacon, lettuce, and tomato? Try using prosciutto and arugula instead, with tomato and Andalusian Mayonnaise (p. 67).

Lamburgers with Andalusian Mayonnaise

Serves 4

Heat the grill. Shape 1½ pounds of lean ground lamb into four 6-ounce patties, sprinkle with coarse salt and freshly ground (or cracked) pepper, and grill until browned on the outside but pink in the center, about 5 minutes per side over hot coals. Serve on thick slices of rye or seven-grain bread that have been rubbed with garlic and grilled. Top with a thick slice of sweet onion if you so desire and a dollop of Andalusian Mayo.

Stewed Tomatoes, Soups, and a Juice

Some Thoughts on Stewed Tomatoes

"*Y*OU just put some olive oil in a pan," said Carol Macleod dreamily, a few weeks before any of her tomatoes had ripened, "and then you add a head or two heads of garlic, smashed and peeled, and when those have given off some of their fragrance after being cooked slowly in the olive oil, you add maybe twenty tomatoes cut up in chunks and you cook those slowly for maybe an hour and a half. Then it's done! Some people, like me, like some croutons on top. Some people, who shall remain nameless, even like a poached egg in it."

The nameless person, we projected, was Carol's husband, Greg, who shares a predilection with James Beard, the great chef. Beard writes of a similar dish that his mother served, cooked tomatoes topped with poached egg (see An Egg Baked in a Tomato, p. 117), and I like this idea, although I grew up with a sweeter tooth.

Rosemary Barron spans the breach in *Flavors of Greece* and calls it salata. It is, like much old-country cooking, both sweet and savory. It comes from the Greek island of Khios and consists of finely chopped onions and tomatoes flavored with cinnamon and garlic and then cooked heartily in olive oil until the tomatoes have given up their moisture. Honey and balsamic vinegar are stirred in, and bowls of it can then be served with a swirl of yogurt and a sprinkling of parsley or coriander. It is somewhere beyond a small salad, similar to our Sautéed Fresh Tomato Sauce (p. 65) and near to the Baked Ratatouille with Lemon Basil Crumbs (p. 126) or stewed tomatoes. Furthermore, there is so little moisture left that it can be stored like the Dried Tomato Harissa (p. 144) in little glass jars with a sealing of olive oil.

Gazpacho

This salad-cum-soup is best if you take the time to dice the vegetables very finely. Some people simply dump everything into a blender, but they miss the pleasure — yes, a time-consuming one — of preparing these soul-satisfying things and eating the tiny dice, which is much more satisfying than slurping a puree. Given garden-fresh produce, don't be limited by the vegetables we list, but use your imagination. Thin wheels of baby okra would be pleasant, or slivers of young leek.

Serves 2 or 3

3 large, absolutely ripe tomatoes (1½ pounds), skinned, gently seeded, and diced

1 red pepper, roasted, skinned, and diced

1 green pepper, roasted, skinned, and diced

1 jalapeño pepper, seeded and minced

1 cucumber, peeled, seeded, and diced

1 large white onion, diced

2 garlic cloves, smashed, peeled, and minced

several torn leaves of basil

juice of 1 lemon

¼ cup very good olive oil

coarse salt and freshly ground pepper to taste

1 cup garlic Croutons (p. 30)

unsweetened thick yogurt

Combine all the ingredients except salt and pepper, Croutons, and yogurt in a large earthenware bowl, and then season to taste. Cover and refrigerate until ready to serve. Correct seasonings. Toss the Croutons in a sauté pan over high heat until they are hot. Serve the soup in bowls with a dollop of yogurt and several Croutons.

Quick Cold Tomato Cream

You're late, late, late. Pick the tomatoes from the garden, chunk 'em in a food processor, then strain through a food mill to remove seeds and skins. From there on out it's smooth sailing.

Serves 4

2 large ripe tomatoes (1 pound)	¾ teaspoon salt
1½ cups Rich Chicken Broth (p. 116)	⅛ teaspoon freshly ground pepper
½ cup Crème Fraîche (p. 56) or heavy cream	1 large tomato, peeled, seeded, and diced
1 teaspoon minced fresh thyme leaves	1 cup Croutons (p. 30)
	4 sprigs of fresh thyme

Chop tomatoes and pass them through a food mill to remove skins and seeds and produce a puree. Stir together all ingredients except the diced tomato, Croutons, and thyme sprigs. Correct seasonings and stir in the diced tomato. If you have the time, you can chill the soup for several hours before serving to allow flavors to mellow. Serve garnished with Croutons and a sprig of fresh thyme.

Chilled North African Soup

We wanted an uncooked tomato soup with a Moroccan flavor. The spices are mellowed in oil and broth over heat, then added to the uncooked tomatoes to make a very striking soup. We've tried decreasing the oil to none, but we like at least a tablespoon. The flavors flower, gorgeous and unexpected.

Serves 4

1 cup Rich Chicken Broth (p. 116)	½ teaspoon hot paprika
1 to 3 tablespoons olive oil	¼ teaspoon ground cumin
1 tablespoon honey	3 large ripe, juicy tomatoes (1½ pounds), crushed
1 teaspoon salt	
2 thin lemon slices	1 tablespoon each minced fresh cilantro and Italian parsley
½ teaspoon crushed caraway seeds	
½ teaspoon cinnamon	thin lemon slices

In a small pot place broth, oil, honey, salt, lemon slices, caraway, cinnamon, hot paprika, and ground cumin. Bring to a simmer over low heat and cook for 15 minutes. Place tomatoes, cilantro, and parsley in a serving bowl or small tureen. Strain and stir hot flavored broth into them. Chill several hours to allow flavors to marry and serve garnished with thin lemon slices.

Flavored Oils

Red Pepper Oil

There is nothing like this to awaken the taste buds and to give a jolt of pure pleasure to dishes like the Yellow Tomato and Pepper Bavarian (p. 101). Or trace a pattern of flavor on top of a cream soup, such as High Summer Soup (p. 120).

Put 2 cups good virgin olive oil and 2 large, meaty red peppers, seeded, membranes removed, and chunked, into a blender or bowl of a food processor and whir until well chopped. Pour into a high-sided skillet and place over medium-low heat for about an hour, or until most of the pepper granules float to the surface. Strain through several thicknesses of dampened cheesecloth. The oil will be distinctly red, but it should not contain very much pulp.

Red Pepper Puree is the resulting puree captured by the cheesecloth. Save this pulp in a squeeze bottle with a coarse tip — I use a bear-shaped plastic bottle that once held honey. This will not keep for more than a week or two unless you freeze it between uses. Try it on bowls of High Summer Soup.

Basil Oil

Heat 2 cups good olive oil until wavy but not yet giving off its

Cream of Tomato and Potato Soup

When it comes to hot soups of this season, it is Elizabeth David's "Potage Crème de Tomates et de Pommes de Terre" that comes to my mind and to which my copy of *French Provincial Cooking* falls open. It is a perfect summer soup; fat leeks are pulled from the soil, cleaned, and wilted in sweet butter, and then tomatoes are crunched up with them, cooked with potatoes, the whole silvered with thick English cream just before chervil is sprinkled over at the end.

"For all its simplicity and cheapness this is a lovely soup, in which you taste butter, cream and each vegetable, and personally, I think it would be a mistake to add anything to it in the way of individual fantasies," cautions David.

We make hers at least once a summer. The rest of the time we make the slimmer version here, not as unctuous, but no less flavorful. The Red Pepper Puree is pure luxury, and as such can be omitted only at the cost of your pleasure. This amount feeds three for supper quite nicely, but can easily be doubled if not tripled.

3 tablespoons olive oil	2 teaspoons salt
2 leeks, white part and tender green, carefully cleaned, sliced thin	several grinds of black pepper
	2 cups whole milk
2 large ripe tomatoes, cored and cut into eighths	4 tablespoons chopped chervil, thyme, or oregano
2 large baking potatoes	Red Pepper Puree
2 teaspoons sugar	Croutons (p. 30)

Heat a large-bottomed saucepan or high-sided sauté pan over medium heat and when it is hot add the olive oil and then the leeks. Stir them with a wooden spoon and when they begin to wilt — lower the heat if need be — add the tomatoes. Let them cook while you scrub and cut the potatoes into small chunks, and when the tomatoes begin to give off their juices, add the potatoes to the pan. Sprinkle with sugar, salt, and pepper, and add about 2 cups of cold water. Turn the heat up a bit, cover the pan, and bring just to a boil, then turn the heat to low and simmer for about 20 minutes or until the potatoes are tender. Cool the mixture a bit, uncovered, and then put through a food mill. Return the puree to the rinsed-out saucepan. Just before serving, stir in the milk and correct the seasonings and just heat through. Stir in the herb, ladle into soup plates, and garnish with a design of the Red Pepper Puree.

scent and remove from heat. Plunge 2 cups cleaned and dried — and packed — basil leaves into the oil, which will bubble up, and clap the top over the pan immediately. Leave to bubble and then steep for 20 minutes. Strain through a fine sieve for some time without pressing. You want to get all the oil you can without any basil pulp, which would eventually spoil. If you find, after letting it set for 24 hours, that the oil is still very cloudy with pulp, you can warm it and let it drain through several thicknesses of dampened cheesecloth. This same technique can be used to make other delicate herbed oils, such as tarragon or marjoram.

Tomato Dill Soup

Dillweed, the feathers from the ferny plant, is quintessentially summer and flavors this soup, which Ruth used to make at her restaurant, La Famille. It is remarkably simple to make, and is not pureed, because we like the texture.

Serves 6

1 tablespoon butter	¼ cup chopped fresh dill
2 tablespoons vegetable oil	1 tablespoon honey
1 medium onion, chopped (1 cup)	1 teaspoon salt
4 large ripe tomatoes (2 pounds), skinned and chopped	¼ teaspoon freshly ground pepper
	sour cream
1½ cups Rich Chicken Broth (p. 116)	freshly chopped dill

Heat butter and oil in a medium-sized pan and sauté the onion until translucent, about 5 minutes. Add tomatoes, Chicken Broth, dill, honey, salt, and pepper and bring to a boil. Lower heat and simmer for about 20 minutes.

Serve hot, with a spoonful of sour cream and a sprinkle of fresh dill.

Sweet Tomatoes' Tuscan Bread Soup

Countries that have lived for centuries in poverty have quite often developed intricate cuisines based on imaginative and almost arcane ways of dealing with simple ingredients. It's a way of coping, an indication of simple joy. Bread has almost always been a basic right, made from the simplest grain, risen in local air, baked in outdoor stones, flavored with herbs picked last minute from underfoot, mixed, sometimes, with broth from a bone, and turned into a salad or soup of often delicious poverty.

Jim Reiman is the owner of Sweet Tomatoes Brick Oven Trattorias in Hanover and Burlington, which serve inspired Italian food, much of it cooked in their wood-burning ovens. There we fell in love with this soup, for which Jim kindly gave us the method.

Serves 8 to 10

8 ounces country-style white bread

8 cups Rich Chicken Broth (p. 116)

1 cup extra-virgin olive oil

4 garlic cloves, smashed, peeled, and chopped

1 bunch of fresh, aromatic sage leaves (½ cup)

2 pounds ripe and juicy tomatoes

salt and pepper

4 tablespoons minced parsley

¼ cup pecorino or Romano cheese, finely grated

Slice the bread in very thin slices and allow to air dry if very fresh, while you bring the broth to a boil in a large saucepan and put sufficient water on to boil to scald the tomatoes for peeling. Heat the oil in a wide-bottomed, high-sided sauté pan over medium heat. Add the garlic and sage leaves and cook until the garlic just begins to color. Add the slices of bread to the oil and fry to golden brown on both sides, tossing gently with a wooden spoon.

After peeling the tomatoes, finely chop them by hand or in a food processor, or put through a food mill directly into the bread mixture after it is browned, and cook for a few minutes, stirring and breaking up some of the crispy browned bread, leaving it chunky, not mushy.

Pour in the boiling broth, taste for seasoning, add salt and pepper as needed, reduce heat, and simmer, covered, for 40 minutes. Correct seasonings.

Just before serving, stir in the parsley. Top each bowl with a sprinkling of cheese.

Herbed Tomato Juice

It is the end of March as we fiddle with some notes on tomato juices, get up, and march down the cellar steps to fetch up a dusty pint jar of Mary Cousineau's dilled tomato juice. The lid is pried off and a spicy fragrance escapes, presaging a taste that is so fresh and shockingly good that it seems as though the essence of summer has been hiding down in the dusty old cellar all these months! Mary Cousineau, Ruth's mother-in-law, taught Ruth how to can and to bake bread, as well as how to grow tomatoes. Mary doesn't stake her tomatoes, but lets them sprawl, then pinches them back, and she always has a great harvest. Homemade juices have a texture and flavor that are nothing like the commercial variety, but don't waste your time making them from any but the finest peak-season tomatoes. In this case we adapted Mary's recipe to the roaster, to make 6 quarts or, of course, 12 pints.

4 pounds very ripe tomatoes, quartered (2 quarts)	3 dill heads, separated into halves (or quarters, for pints)
8 pounds ripe plum tomatoes, quartered (4 quarts)	3 teaspoons sugar 3 teaspoons salt

Preheat oven to 400 degrees. Wash the tomatoes, quarter them, put them in a broiler pan, and place in the oven for 45 minutes to an hour, or until the tomatoes are very tender and have squashed down upon themselves. They will be browned on the tops. Take them from the oven, let them cool a bit, and put them through a food mill to remove seeds and skins.

Scald 6 quart or 12 pint canning jars, lids, and rings. For quart jars, place half a dill head in each (¼ dill head in each pint), along with ½ teaspoon each (¼ teaspoon each for pints) of sugar and salt. Stir tomato juice with a ladle, and fill jars, leaving 1 inch headroom. Seal and process 10 minutes in a boiling water bath. Cool and store in a dark, cool place.

Variation: You may substitute basil, thyme, tarragon, savory, lovage, or another favorite herb, or combination of herbs, for the dill.

Vegetable Dishes

Cilantro, Jalapeño, and Tomato Rice

$\mathcal{I}$T'S hard to believe that cilantro was a new, if intriguing, taste a few years ago, at least to those who had not visited Mexico or the Orient. We don't know what we ever did without it. We particularly like it combined with mint and hot pepper in this recipe.

Serves 4 to 6 as a side dish

2 large ripe tomatoes
  (1 pound), peeled,
  seeded, and coarsely
  chopped
2 garlic cloves, smashed,
  peeled, and minced
1 small red onion,
  peeled and cut into
  small shards
1 jalapeño pepper (or to
  taste), chopped

1 cup chopped fresh
  mint
1 cup chopped fresh
  cilantro
2 tablespoons red wine
  vinegar
2 tablespoons olive oil
1½ teaspoons salt
1 cup long-grain basmati
  rice
1 teaspoon salt

Combine tomatoes, garlic, onion, pepper, mint, cilantro, vinegar, oil, and salt in a large crockery bowl, set aside, and let the flavors blend for about 1 hour.

In the meantime, cook the rice. Bring 2 cups cold water to a boil in a 1-quart pot. Add the salt and stir in the rice. Cover the pot and lower the heat to very low. Simmer, covered, for 20 minutes, or until all the water has been absorbed. Toss hot rice with the cool dressing and allow to marinate until it is room temperature.

Basil Broth Risotto

Fresh, fresh, fresh, with a basil-scented chicken broth, succulent tomatoes chunked and stirred into the creamy, basil-scented rice at the very end. Be sure to use the short, starchy arborio rice in this dish. You could serve this with the grilled chicken breasts that you have boned to make the broth (see directions for broth in Chicken, Shrimp, and Buttermilk Pie, p. 170), or you could replace the chicken broth with a good vegetable one.

Serves 4 to 6

1 quart good chicken broth, defatted	coarse salt
30 basil leaves, cleaned	coarsely ground pepper
2 tablespoons olive oil	2 large ripe, juicy, flavorful tomatoes (1 pound)
1 garlic clove, smashed, peeled, and minced	Parmesan shavings
1 shallot, peeled and chopped	
1 cup arborio rice	

Bring the broth to a boil, then lower the heat to keep it at a simmer. Tear half the clean basil leaves into it. Put a medium-sized saucepan over medium heat, add the olive oil, and stir in the garlic and shallot. Allow to cook for about 2 minutes and then stir in the rice and a little more olive oil if needed to coat it. Stir in a ladleful of broth and keep stirring, intermittently. Watch the pan and stir it as though you were watching a baby while peeling potatoes. When most of the broth has been absorbed, add another ladleful and stir it in. Continue until all the broth has been added. Meanwhile, core the tomatoes, halve and lightly seed, then chop roughly. When all the broth has been absorbed

Vegetable Broth

Many people are in the habit of using a meat broth automatically for a soup, but for a vegetable soup it is appropriate to make a nicely flavored vegetable broth by simmering the parings and/or skins and/or roots of many vegetables in a sufficient amount of water until it is flavorful, and then straining it. Potato peelings are neutrally and earthily flavorful, as are pea pods, mushrooms, onion skins, and tomatoes. Add some wine. It can be flavored with parsley, basil, bay leaves, marjoram, savory, lovage, or celery, and then strained to be used as you like.

Tomato Broth

You can make a fresh tomato broth by chopping 4 to 6 pounds of tomatoes in the food processor with a handful of parsley leaves until they are pureed. Put them in a pan and bring to a fast simmer over medium heat. Simmer about 10 minutes or until all the juices have had a chance to escape from softened cell walls. Toward the end of that cooking you can add a handful of chopped basil leaves, celery seed, celery leaves, or lovage. But keep it simple. Strain this well through a fine-mesh strainer and discard the pulp. You can use the broth as the basis of a soup, sauce, or vinaigrette. We like to use it to poach a fish or steam vegetables and then use it as a broth, perhaps slightly reduced.

The Combination

A combination of meat and vegetable essences is described by George Lang in his definitive The Cuisine of Hungary. *There, an intriguing white tomato soup involves simmering a ratio of 1 ripe peeled tomato to each cup of strong chicken broth for an hour and then straining all the tomato from the broth. Is there any reason this wouldn't be just as good if not better with a good beef broth?*

by the rice and it is creamy, correct the seasonings, tear the rest of the basil leaves into the rice, and stir in the fresh tomatoes. Garnish with curls of Parmesan and serve immediately.

Fried Ripe Tomatoes with Mozzarella and Basil

One sumptuous way of sautéing ripe tomatoes is Edouard de Pomiane's, as quoted by Elizabeth David in *An Omelet and a Glass of Wine*. In a delicate, sensuous process, small ripe tomatoes are cut in half and very slowly sautéed in butter over low heat while the plump sides of the tomatoes are pricked to let the juices run. They are turned and sautéed, then turned again and then again, and thick, sweet cream is poured over them and whisked into the juices.

The following are unthinkably voluptuous as well, so near yet so far from Fried Green Tomatoes (p. 25) and from de Pomiane's above.

Cut firm, small, ripe, meaty tomatoes into eighths. Dredge them in a good, strong, unbleached flour — or fine corn flour to give a very crispy finish — seasoned with salt and pepper. Fry them in a mixture of butter and oil over medium heat just until browned. Keep moving them carefully to brown on all sides before they become mushy. Garnish with some basil leaves — for the scent — and serve with a hunk of crusty bread and butter and some fresh mozzarella. This satisfies all the senses.

Three Fishes with Ripe Tomatoes

Spinach and Salmon Cakes with Tomato Dill Sauce

I don't believe that this recipe had any tomatoes in it when it was handed to me in Vermont by my sister Sal on her way back from a visit to our mother, Beth, in Michigan, to her own home in Maine. I immediately thought it needed fresh tomatoes and incorporated them. Ruth then made some of her own changes, and now it's absolutely perfect. And to think this is salmon from a can, which is something I detested when I was a kid on account of the bones; be sure to mash up those bones well. In the unlikely event of leftovers, grill or toast good, thickly cut fresh bread, mash a salmon cake with a dollop of sauce on it, top with a shaving of Swiss cheese (or not), and run under the broiler.

Serves 4

For the cakes:

1½ pounds fresh
   spinach, rinsed until
   the water runs clean
   (or 1 10-ounce
   package frozen)
1 can salmon
   (7½ ounces)
1 egg
½ cup minced onion
1 medium tomato
   (5 ounces), peeled,
   seeded, and chopped

1 tablespoon minced
   fresh dill
1 tablespoon minced
   fresh parsley
½ teaspoon salt
⅛ teaspoon freshly
   ground pepper
1½ cups dry Bread
   Crumbs (p. 90)
1 tablespoon butter
2 tablespoons vegetable
   oil

For the sauce:

1 tablespoon butter
1 tablespoon flour
1½ cups milk
1 medium tomato
   (5 ounces), peeled,
   seeded, and chopped
1 tablespoon minced
   fresh dill

1 tablespoon minced
   fresh parsley
½ teaspoon salt
⅛ teaspoon freshly
   ground pepper
2 teaspoons lemon juice

In a large sauté pan cook the fresh spinach in the water that clings to the leaves after washing, just until limp. Cool. Squeeze out liquid, chop fine, and put it in a large bowl. Do not cook frozen spinach, just thaw and squeeze out excess liquid before chopping. Drain the salmon and reserve the liquid. Mash the salmon with a fork, paying particular attention to the bones, and add to the spinach. Stir in egg, onion, tomato, dill, parsley, salt, pepper, and ½ cup of Bread Crumbs. Mix well and form into 8 cakes. Place the remaining Bread Crumbs on a plate and coat the cakes with the crumbs. In a large skillet, heat the butter and

oil and brown cakes on both sides. Remove to an ovenproof platter, cover loosely with foil, and place in a low oven to keep warm
while you make the sauce.

To make the sauce, add the butter to the skillet and melt.
Whisk in the flour and cook for 1 minute. Add the milk and reserved salmon liquid and bring to a boil over medium heat, stirring constantly until smooth. Add tomato, herbs, salt, and
pepper, and cook until nicely thickened, about 5 minutes. Stir in
the lemon juice.

Serve 2 cakes, napped with some sauce, per person.

White Fish with Tomato Concassée

"Concassée" is a fancy French word for tomatoes that have been skinned, cut in half, gently seeded and juiced, and then diced quite small, to be used in many, many dishes. It's one of the first things we do when tomato season strikes. You can use haddock or scrod or sole for this dish, but orange roughy or good red snapper is great.

Serves 4 to 6

3 tablespoons extra-virgin olive oil
1 to 1½ pounds white fish
2 garlic cloves, smashed, peeled, and chopped
½ white onion, chopped (⅓ cup)
½ sweet red pepper, peeled and slivered
chopped hot pepper to taste

1 large, plump, red tomato (8 ounces), peeled, seeded, and diced
5 oil-cured black olives, smashed, pitted, and chopped coarsely
1 small bunch of parsley
coarse salt
freshly ground pepper
½ cup Bread Crumbs (p. 90)

Preheat oven to 425 degrees. With a portion of the olive oil, lavishly oil a medium-sized baking dish, into which the fish should be placed in a single layer. Mix garlic, onion, red pepper, hot pepper, tomato, and olives and strew over the fish. Chop the parsley and strew half of it over the fish and toss half of it with the Bread Crumbs. Sprinkle the fish with salt and pepper to taste, strew with the Bread Crumb mixture, and drizzle with remaining oil. Bake for 15 minutes, or until fish separates with a fork and top is browned.

Variation: To mellow the flavors of the garlic, onion, red pepper, and hot pepper, sauté them briefly over medium-low heat just until wilted before sprinkling over the fish.

Grilled Swordfish Agrodolce

Sweet and tart, this Sicilian sauce can be made ahead of time for an elegant meal of grilled swordfish. Neither the hearty fish nor the sauce will overpower the other. The sauce would be tasty on grilled tuna as well. Best with fried or grilled polenta.

Serves 2

2 tablespoons fruity olive oil plus more for brushing on swordfish

6 anchovy fillets, rinsed and chopped

1 cup sliced onion

2 garlic cloves, smashed, peeled, and finely chopped

1 tablespoon fresh rosemary needles or 1 teaspoon dried

2 cups chopped tomatoes

2 tablespoons balsamic vinegar

1 tablespoon light brown sugar

1 tablespoon pitted, chopped oil-cured black olives

1 tablespoon capers

1 tablespoon minced parsley

pinch of salt

⅛ teaspoon freshly ground pepper

⅔ pound swordfish (⅓ pound per person)

fresh herbs

Start the coals. Meanwhile, heat oil and sauté the anchovies, onion, garlic, and rosemary in a medium-sized skillet over medium heat until onion is wilted and lightly golden, about 10 minutes. Stir in tomatoes and cook, stirring occasionally, for 10 minutes. Mix vinegar and sugar together and add to skillet. Stir well and cook another 10 minutes. Stir in olives, capers, parsley, salt, and pepper. Remove from heat and cover to keep warm while grilling the fish. If made ahead, reheat over low flame while fish is grilling.

Brush the fish with oil and sprinkle with salt and freshly ground pepper. Grill fish 3 minutes on each side per 1-inch thickness. The fish should be moist and feel firm to the touch. Put on a serving dish and spoon warm sauce over it. Garnish with sprigs of fresh herbs.

Breads

Tomato Upside-Down Cornbread

THE idea for this came from my family's traditional birthday hankering for pineapple upside-down cakes. We wanted a corny bread that was topped — upside-down-style — with a savory tomato and garlic caramel. It is an intriguing way to pair those so compatible tastes of cornmeal and tomato. A cup or two of corn kernels added to the batter adds panache.

Makes 10 hearty wedges

For the topping:

3 tablespoons vegetable oil

1 tablespoon chopped fresh oregano or 1 teaspoon dried

2 garlic cloves, smashed, peeled, and minced

2 large ripe tomatoes, cored and thinly sliced

½ teaspoon each salt and freshly ground pepper

For the batter:

1 cup yellow cornmeal
1 cup all-purpose flour
  (4 ounces)
⅛ cup granulated sugar
1 tablespoon baking
  powder
1 teaspoon salt
½ teaspoon freshly
  ground pepper, or to
  taste
1 jalapeño pepper,
  seeded and minced

1 clove garlic, smashed,
  peeled, and minced
1 small onion or shallot,
  minced
½ cup cheddar cheese,
  grated
1 egg
1 cup milk
⅓ cup vegetable oil

Preheat the oven to 400 degrees. Place a 10-inch black cast-iron skillet over medium heat, and when it is hot add the oil. Sprinkle with half the oregano, then the garlic, then make a spiral of overlapping tomato slices to cover the bottom of the pan. Sprinkle with the salt and pepper. Turn the heat to medium low and heat the tomatoes while you prepare the batter.

Combine the cornmeal, flour, sugar, baking powder, and salt and pepper in a mixing bowl. Add the jalapeño, garlic, onion, remaining oregano, and cheese and toss. In a small bowl whisk together the egg, milk, and oil and stir into the dry ingredients.

Pull the pan from the heat and carefully dot the batter over the tomatoes, smoothing and filling without disturbing the tomatoes. Bake for 30 minutes, or until a straw inserted in the center comes out clean.

Using as many pot holders as you need, carefully place a large plate over the pan and flip. Let the pan rest over the cake on the plate for 15 minutes before serving. Replace any of the topping that sticks to the bottom of the pan. Serve at once.

Bruschetta

Bruschetta is essentially made with a good white Italian or French bread — dense, but not so chewy that it becomes hard when ¾-inch slices of it are grilled crispy on the outside while the inside remains soft. The slices are then rubbed with a smashed and peeled clove of garlic, a process that leaves much of the garlic behind, and then with a halved, meaty, ripe tomato, which is gently squeezed so that it leaves behind little bits of itself. Half a meaty tomato will disintegrate in this way. You can drizzle this with a few drops of fruity olive oil and another few drops of red wine vinegar.

Another time, after the bread is grilled and rubbed with a peeled clove of garlic and drizzled, or not, with good olive oil, the Bruschetta may be topped with anchovies or olives or, best of all, with Espey's Basic Salsa (p. 57).

Bread Crumbs

Take advantage of any stale heels of bread to break them into the bowl of the food processor and process into crumbs. Store them in a plastic bag in the freezer, using them and adding to them as needed. The crumbs can be toasted by putting them in a 350-degree oven for 10 to 15 minutes.

Flavored Bread Crumbs

Add a clove or two of garlic, salt, coarsely ground pepper, parsley, or the herb(s) of your choice, a shallot, an onion, even a grating of nutmeg if you like, to be processed along with half a baguette of bread. Freeze and use as needed, but store the next batch of crumbs separately.

Part 3

Peak of the Season

SWING GENTLY IN THAT garden hammock — sip a cool drink — any-time expect a tiger to creep through that jungle of peak season.

Tomato is surrounded. Okra's luscious flowers, of the hibiscus family, foretell, with their patterns, the cut okra pod, but when that fruit appears it has the peculiar ability to hide on its tall, sparsely leaved stalk. Not until you peer for the pods from different points of view do they suddenly appear. Under the large leaves of the eggplant, droopy, velvety purple flowers hang, suddenly ceding to the bulbous weight of the fruit; and peppers, pining for heat and the correct amount of moisture, elongate and turn from green to streaked to red, while tiny hot peppers explode in prickles of red across their mother plants. Fennel's leafy fronds tickle tough leek spears, while below them both their sumptuous roots escape luminous and fat from the earth. And then the herbs — summer's precious days are being meted out and cel-ebrated by such as basil, whose fragrance perfumes your dooryard on this particular July day.

Black Cat unwinds from his lair among the melons to wend around your hanging feet, and you sigh and push back, reaching for your garden gloves. Summer . . .

Appetizers and First Courses

Mexican Pumpkin-Seed Dip

*H*ERE we roast the tomato, as we do many times throughout this book, to produce a different, deep, sweet meaty taste. Although it was no doubt a combination of influences that prodded us to do this, perhaps it was initially Diana Kennedy's recipe for a pumpkin-seed dip called *sikil'p'ak*. Included in *Recipes from the Regional Cooks of Mexico*, this blissfully intriguing combination of ingredients, which we've adapted from the original, seemed to call for roasting. You roast and grind the pumpkin seeds, roast and chop the peppers and tomatoes, then stir everything together. You can use whatever fresh hot chiles you can find, but we like the flavor of the carrot-sized, glossy, thick-walled New Mexican. This dip can be spread on Bruschetta (p. 90) or scooped up on leaves of endive or toasted corn or flour tortillas or pita bread. Thin it with a little olive oil and use as a sauce for green beans or broccoli.

Makes about 2½ cups

3 tablespoons olive oil	3 ripe tomatoes (about
1 cup pumpkin seeds	12 ounces)
1½ teaspoons salt, or	2 tablespoons each
more to taste	chopped cilantro and
2 fresh New Mexican	chives
chiles	

Heat a medium-sized, heavy-bottomed sauté pan over medium heat and when it is hot add the olive oil. When the oil is wavy hot, pour in the pumpkin seeds and toss until coated. Sprinkle with the salt and toss. Turn the heat to medium or very low and cook, stirring often, until the pumpkin seeds are brown. If the heat is too high, the seeds will pop like corn and may burn. When they are crisp and brown, set them aside to cool. Then grind them to a coarse powder in a mortar or food processor and transfer to a small bowl.

Meanwhile, under a broiler or over a grill, roast and skin the chiles. When the chiles are roasted, remove from the broiler, turn it off, and set oven to 450 degrees. Roast the tomatoes for about 20 minutes, turning every so often, until soft and browned, then slide off the skins. Grind the tomatoes and half the chiles together in a blender or food processor. Chop the rest of the chiles very fine. Stir the tomatoes, cilantro, chives, and chiles to taste into the pumpkin seeds. Correct the seasonings. Serve at room temperature.

Avocado Filled with Lime-Pickled Shrimp

What could be more refreshing, beautiful, and delicious than sitting indolently beneath the spread of a maple tree with friends, thinking about weeding the garden but nibbling on this instead?

Serves 4

1 pound medium shrimp	⅔ cup peeled, seeded, and diced tomatoes
½ cup freshly squeezed lime juice (about 4 limes)	1½ tablespoons seeded and finely chopped fresh jalapeño pepper
1 teaspoon salt	
½ teaspoon toasted cumin seeds, crushed (or 1/4 teaspoon ground cumin)	2 ripe avocados
	spinach or arugula leaves
¼ cup chopped red onion	

Bring a pot of water to a boil. Add shrimp and cook just 45 seconds. The shells will turn pink immediately. Drain and plunge into ice water to stop them from cooking further. Drain again and peel.

Place the shrimp in a glass bowl and cover with lime juice, salt, and cumin. Marinate 1 hour. Add onion, tomatoes, and jalapeño and let sit half an hour before serving.

Peel and slice avocados. Divide the greens among four plates, and divide the avocado slices evenly among them. Spoon the shrimp mixture over the avocados with a bit of the lime marinade.

Garlic Custards on Kale with Tomato Vinaigrette

Consider these tiny creamy custards as condiments, classic spoonfuls to bring out the jazz of tomatoey kale. Or give them a life of their own by baking them in partially baked hollowed-out pattypan squash, halved tomatoes, or small, round Italian eggplants.

Serves 4; can easily be doubled

For the custards:

3 garlic cloves, smashed and peeled	**½ teaspoon salt**
1 cup heavy cream	**1 large egg plus 1 yolk**

Simmer garlic, cream, and salt together in a heavy saucepan over low heat for 15 minutes. Remove from heat and let steep for another 15 minutes. Heat oven to 350 degrees. Beat the egg and yolk together in a small bowl and strain the cream mixture into the eggs to remove the garlic. Blend well. Pour into 4 small greased custard cups or ramekins. Place cups in a baking pan and place on oven rack. Pour enough hot water into the pan to come halfway up the cups. Bake 25 minutes or until custards are set. Remove them from the water and let cool for 15 minutes before unmolding.

For the Tomato Vinaigrette:

½ cup tomato puree
1½ tablespoons balsamic
   vinegar
½ tablespoon honey
3 tablespoons olive oil

¼ teaspoon salt
¼ teaspoon pepper
½ tablespoon minced
   shallot

Whisk all ingredients together until well blended.

For the kale:

1 pound kale, washed   2 tablespoons olive oil

Tear kale leaves from stems and coarsely shred. Bring a large pot of salted water to the boil and blanch the kale for 4 minutes. Drain, refresh in cold water, and squeeze to remove excess moisture. Heat the oil in a large skillet and sauté the kale to heat through. Divide the kale among 4 small serving plates and nap with the Tomato Vinaigrette. Run a knife around each of the custards to release them from the molds and turn them out onto the kale. Drizzle with a little more vinaigrette.

Ruth's Biscuit Pizza

Once upon a time, a small friend — a very picky eater — consented to come to dinner with her mother because we were having pizza. But woe betook her when she realized that this pizza did not come in a box, but was being baked on the grill and was topped with thin, crescent-shaped slices of seeded and juiced tomato, along with garlic and onion (no anchovies that night), Parmesan cheese sprinkled over, and a drizzle of olive oil. Another one — for adults only — was topped with (horrors!) zucchini and eggplant and okra, as well as tomatoes, before being grilled. They could as easily have been baked, but in the summer I think it's great to grill them. The best specific directions for doing so can be found in Johanne Killeen and George Germon's *Cucina Simpatica,* which is a lovely book for pastas and all kinds of grilled foods.

We experimented with such a continuum of pizzas and tarts and biscuit pies that one day Ruth went home and, thinking pizza, came up with a biscuit pizza in her own inimitable style — bright, colorful, and full of flavor. As she was making it, she remembered one of her friend François Dinand's *trucs* of the trade, and sprinkled semolina over the crust before putting in the filling — to absorb the juices and prevent a soggy crust. Although this crust is crunchy, it is also tender, and with its mellow topping would not take kindly to grilling. We like the combination of French tricks and American biscuitry. Serve as an appetizer or a snack.

Serves 8

For the crust:

1 teaspoon minced garlic	1½ teaspoons baking powder
¼ cup olive oil	½ teaspoon salt
¼ cup milk	½ teaspoon freshly ground pepper
1 cup all-purpose flour	

For the topping:

2 tablespoons olive oil	½ teaspoon salt
1 cup sliced onion	⅛ teaspoon pepper
1 cup sliced red pepper	¼ cup freshly grated Parmesan cheese
1 cup sliced yellow pepper	2 tablespoons semolina
½ teaspoon minced garlic	3 to 4 ripe tomatoes thickly sliced into 10 slices
1 heaping teaspoon fresh rosemary needles	

Preheat the oven to 425 degrees. Steep the garlic in the oil and milk over low heat for 10 minutes. Stir flour, baking powder, salt, and pepper together in bowl. Stir the milk mixture into the flour to make a soft dough. Pat out a 12-inch circle on an ungreased cookie sheet with floured fingertips. The crust will be less than ¼ inch thick.

For the topping, heat the oil in a large skillet over medium heat and sauté the onion, peppers, garlic, and rosemary together about 15 to 20 minutes, stirring occasionally, just to soften. Season with salt and pepper.

Mix the cheese and semolina together and sprinkle over the crust, leaving a 1-inch border. Top with a single layer of tomato slices. Spoon sautéed mixture over the tomatoes and bake 20 to 25 minutes until crust is golden brown. Serve warm.

Tomato Crème Fraîche Tart

"Oh, you have to try Stevie's Tomato Basil Tart," said our friend Kathleen Patten when she heard we were writing this book. Stevie and Kathleen live way out in the boonies near Hinesburg, Vermont, in houses separated by the extensive gardens from which most of the ingredients for Stevie's tart are gathered.

Serves 8 as a first course

1 recipe Italian Butter
   Pastry (p. 35), chilled
   for 1 hour
2 tablespoons semolina
2 large ripe tomatoes
   (1 pound), sliced

1 cup Crème Fraîche
   (p. 56)
2 tablespoons minced
   fresh basil
½ teaspoon salt
⅛ teaspoon pepper

Preheat oven to 425 degrees. Roll out crust on a well-floured surface and fit into a 10-inch tart pan with a removable bottom. Sprinkle semolina over the crust and put a single layer of tomato slices over that, slightly overlapping them. Season the Crème Fraîche with basil, salt, and pepper and spoon over the tomatoes. Bake 30 to 35 minutes, until the crust is golden brown and the top of the tart is bubbling and brown. Serve warm.

Salads, Salsas, and Sauces

Yellow Tomato and Pepper Bavarian

A golden, voluptuous accompaniment to hot grilled meats or as the centerpiece of a salad in small amounts or even scooped into the middle of a hot or cold soup to melt or chill, this classy "Jell-O" can be set in an oiled, four-cup decorative mold if you wish to serve it on a buffet table surrounded by spicy greens, or surround it with wilted greens such as the Kale with Tomato Vinaigrette on p. 96. Make individual salads by scooping it out onto spicy arugula or watercress, then drizzle it with Red Pepper Oil or Red Pepper Puree thinned with a little fruity olive oil, or with Basil Oil (pp. 73–74).

Serves 8

2 medium yellow tomatoes (1 pound), coarsely chopped	1 small sprig of basil
	1 envelope plain gelatin
	½ teaspoon salt
1 large yellow pepper (8 ounces), seeded and coarsely chopped	4 dashes of hot pepper sauce
	1 cup heavy cream

Place tomatoes, pepper, and basil in a small pot. Add gelatin and salt, cover, and simmer over medium heat for 10 minutes or until vegetables are tender. Puree through a food mill to remove

101

skins and seeds. Cool, then stir in hot pepper sauce. You will have about 2 cups. Whip cream, fold in puree, and chill until firm, about 2 hours.

Lemonlime and Tomato Aspic

Our friend Peder Johnson had two suggestions when the *Tomato Imperative!* newsletter came out — he remembered with fondness his mother's tomato aspic and a tomato pudding. For the former, she combined commercially canned tomatoes, peppers, and onions with a box of lemon Jell-O. We found another sweet tomato jelly in a book from the Ladies of the Golden Rule Circle in Swanton, Vermont. It was made the same way, then chilled in a shallow pan, cut into squares, and served in lettuce leaves with a mayonnaise. A handwritten recipe in an anonymous recipe index detailed a savory version — tomato aspic salad made of unflavored gelatin, condensed tomato soup, lemon juice, and mustard, as well as finely diced vegetables. All these things considered, we came up with the following aspic, which we allow to set in a ring mold. Eat it with roasted chicken breasts or fill with your favorite chicken salad.

Serves about 6

1½ cups Roasted Tomato and Vegetable Sauce (p. 110)	juice of 1 lemon
	juice of 1 lime
2 cups Rich Chicken Broth (p. 116)	2 envelopes plain gelatin (2 tablespoons)
1 tablespoon sugar	½ cup diced celery
1 teaspoon salt	½ cup peeled, seeded, and diced cucumber
2 teaspoons minced fresh tarragon leaves	¼ cup diced green pepper
1 teaspoon lemon zest, in strips	1 tablespoon minced onion

In a quart saucepan, bring tomato sauce, 1¾ cups of Chicken Broth, sugar, salt, and half the tarragon to a boil. Put remaining tarragon, lemon zest, juices, and remaining broth in a bowl and sprinkle the gelatin over to soften. Stir the hot tomato broth mixture into the cold mixture and stir in the vegetables, then pour into an oiled 6-cup mold. Chill. Stir after each half hour to keep vegetables suspended until the aspic starts to jell seriously, about 1¼ hours. Unmold by dipping the mold in hot water briefly and inverting on a serving plate.

Peppy Slaw

We used Sandy Lincoln's Red Hot Pepper Vinegar in this dish. The slaw is tart and piquant, to go wonderfully well with fried chicken, as well as in or with several of the sandwich suggestions on pp. 66–68.

Makes about 4 cups

2 cups shredded cabbage	**3 tablespoons Red Hot Pepper Vinegar**
1 cup diced and seeded ripe tomatoes	**1 tablespoon minced parsley**
½ teaspoon salt	

Toss all ingredients together in a bowl and let stand several hours before serving.

Potato and Arugula Salad

If you love the unctuous, peppery taste of arugula as much as we do, this may make your toes curl with pleasure. This is not your mom's potato salad. For this you need a garden full of herbs and edible flowers to wander around in, picking and picking, or at least a good source for mixed herbs and greens. We like to use lettuce and spinach, a few leaves of radicchio for color, sorrel for bite, then bits of sage, garlic chives, thyme, violet leaves, beet thinnings, parsley, cilantro, and/or chervil — any combination — in addition to a good double handful of arugula and one of mint. The garnish of whole baby tomatoes and nasturtium leaves is gorgeous. The inspiration came from that marvelous book by Viana La Place, *Verdura*.

Serves 6 to 8

1 quart mixed greens
1 large (double) handful of arugula
1 smaller bunch of mint
2 very ripe tomatoes, gently seeded and diced
2 cloves garlic, smashed and peeled
juice of 1 lemon
⅓ cup very fruity virgin olive oil

freshly ground black pepper
2 pounds starchy russet potatoes
salt
1 stem of lovage (or 1 stalk of celery with leaves), chopped
2 large shallots, peeled and sliced thin
½ cup Basic Mayonnaise (p. 66)

Garnish:

1 dozen red, yellow, and pink cherry and/or tiny plum tomatoes with stems

1 dozen nasturtium leaves
1 dozen nasturtium buds or flowers

Wash and dry greens, saving out half the arugula and half the mint. Toss the mixed greens with the tomatoes in a glass serving bowl big enough to hold the finished salad. Chop 1 clove of garlic and whisk with the lemon and olive oil, together with ample grindings of pepper (no salt, as it will wilt greens), and dress the greens with ⅓ to ½ of the dressing, reserving the rest. Cover the greens and chill.

Scrub the potatoes, quarter lengthwise, slice thickly, put in a pan, cover with cold water, add 3 tablespoons of salt and the other clove of garlic, bring to a boil over high heat, reduce heat to medium, and cook until quite tender. Drain and place in a large mixing bowl and let cool for 10 minutes or until still warm but not steaming. Add the lovage and shallots. Tear the reserved arugula and mint over the potatoes. In a small bowl, whisk together the mayonnaise with the reserved oil and lemon mixture. Thin with more oil or lemon juice to taste. Correct seasonings of salt and pepper. Pour over the potatoes and toss lightly but thoroughly with two forks. Taste for seasonings again, then mound over the chilled greens. Around and up the base of the mound but not obscuring the greens, press the nasturtium leaves, flowers, and baby tomatoes. Serve immediately, or chill and serve cold.

Lentil Salad with Feta

Brunoise is the method of cutting vegetables into a tiny, tiny dice by first slicing, stacking the slices and slicing them thin, and then cutting the strips crosswise into dice. It is also the finished result. Your aim should be vegetables that are not much bigger than each lentil, looking like a mass of glistening jewels when mixed with the earth tones of lentils and varnished with fruity olive oil. Lentils cook very quickly, with no soaking, so that they keep their shape and texture. If you have an Indian store near you, it's fun to experiment with different kinds of lentils — called dal — and vegetables. Don't feel you're limited to our favorites here. Only the tomato and the feta, which are added last, are not at all optional. You should taste a grain or two of salty, tangy feta with each bite.

Serves 6 to 8

1 sweet, meaty red
   pepper
2 links chorizo sausage
1 cup lentils, uncooked,
   picked over under
   running cold water
salt and pepper to taste
1 large carrot, pared and
   cut in ¼-inch dice
1 fennel stalk, tender
   parts only, cut in
   ¼-inch dice
1 celery stalk, trimmed,
   cut in ¼-inch dice
1 small white onion,
   chopped

2 garlic cloves, smashed,
   peeled, and minced
2 tablespoons chopped
   fresh cilantro
2 tablespoons chopped
   fresh parsley
3 tablespoons red wine
   vinegar
6 tablespoons fruity
   olive oil
2 medium-sized meaty
   tomatoes, seeded and
   chopped
1 cup feta cheese

Prepare the vegetables just before they are to be used so they don't lose their crispness. With a good vegetable peeler, pare the shiny skin off the red pepper, cut in half vertically through the core, flatten, and slide a flexible, sharp knife over the inside of the pepper to cut away the white pith, seeds, and ribs. Cut in ¼-inch strips, then in ¼-inch dice, and place in a large bowl. Cut the sausage in very small dice and brown in a skillet over medium-low heat until the reddish fat is rendered out and the sausage is slightly browned and crisp, then drain on a paper towel before adding to the bowl with the peppers.

Wipe out the skillet, add the cleaned lentils and 2¼ cups cold water, and when they come to a boil over high heat, immediately turn the heat to low, cover, and simmer just until the lentils are crisp/tender, about 20 minutes. Take them from the heat, season them with coarse salt and freshly ground pepper to taste, add the carrot and fennel, cover, and let steam for 5 minutes off the heat. After 5 minutes, the carrot should still be crisp but just slightly tender. Uncover and chill for 1 hour.

Toss the celery, onion, garlic, cilantro, and parsley in the bowl with the chorizo and pepper. Stir in the vinegar and olive oil and the cooled lentil mixture. Toss and correct seasonings. Chill for several hours. When you are ready to serve, add the tomatoes and toss. Taste for seasonings and crumble an ample amount of feta over the top of the bowl. Pass more crumbled feta for people to help themselves.

Roasted Plain Tomato Sauce

We make this sauce especially to use in Dale's Salsa, which follows, but it can also be packed in small jars to use in stews and other dishes that benefit from a concentrated tomato taste. Make it with peak August tomatoes, before cooler weather makes them acidy and watery. A tool called a Victorio Strainer is great for pureeing big batches of tomatoes and other vegetables, but neither of us owns one. So we make use of a food processor in conjunction with the food mill.

Makes 4 half-pints

12 pounds tomatoes

Core and halve the tomatoes and put them in a deep pan over medium heat. Without stirring bring them to a simmer and cook until the water is released, about 1 hour. Preheat the oven to 375 degrees. Pour the water off the tomatoes, puree in the bowl of a food processor if needed, and then put them through a food mill to remove skins and seeds. Pour the resulting pulp into a roasting pan and place in the oven. Stirring occasionally, roast the tomatoes until reduced to about 1 quart, approximately 1 hour.

Preserve half-pint jars of sauce in a boiling water bath for 20 minutes for a powerful wallop of tomato taste. Or use it all in Dale's Salsa.

Dale's Salsa

Wandering around the farmers' market one day looking for the subject for a column, I began to ask vendors for favorite recipes that used their own produce. I came to Dale and Sandy Lincoln, who grow a cornucopia of handsome organic produce. Sandy makes and markets beautiful, imaginative vinegars, and Dale is a prize-winning amateur cook, famed for his salsa. I asked him his technique and then I went home and got busy. Using the cooked sauce to thicken and sweeten the raw ingredients is Dale's inventive technique, as is ladling out the excess liquid, and he uses a slug of Sandy's Red Hot Pepper Vinegar at the end.

In lieu of the harissa you may substitute a half teaspoon each of cumin and dried coriander and perhaps another hot pepper. You might want to add a minimum number of hot peppers, letting them develop their flavor in the mixture for an adequate time before deciding if you need more fire. Sure, you may can this in a boiling water bath if you're quick about it; otherwise, be warned, it disappears quickly. After eating a bit, I've never been able to can more than 3 pints, but Ruth says that if we didn't eat so much, we could can 8 pints.

8 to 10 ripe red tomatoes (4 pounds), cored, halved, and seeded

5 large, meaty sweet peppers (1½ pounds) of assorted colors, cored, halved, and seeded

3 large, sharp white onions, peeled and halved

2 *heads* of garlic, smashed and peeled

3 to 4 large jalapeños or other hot peppers, or

to taste, cored, halved, and seeded

2 tablespoons salt

2 to 3 tablespoons Dried Tomato Harissa (p. 144)

1 quart Roasted Plain Tomato Sauce (p. 108)

1 cup good vinegar — cider, red wine, or white wine

1 large bunch of cilantro (4 ounces), stemmed and chopped

Chop the tomatoes, peppers, onions, garlic, and jalapeños in small batches either with a food processor or by hand. Don't turn them to mush. Put into a large mixing bowl. Sprinkle with the salt, stir well, then set aside for half an hour. Press a large, bowl-shaped sieve or colander down into the mixture and ladle into a large pan the liquid that has formed. Reduce over medium heat to a syrup, then stir in the raw vegetables, along with the Harissa, the Roasted Plain Tomato Sauce, and the vinegar and bring just to a simmer. Remove from heat; correct the salt and pepper seasonings. Now is the time to add more jalapeño, bit by bit, if you like. I found that the hotness diminished when I canned the salsa.

Roasted Tomato and Vegetable Sauce

In the first edition of *Tomato Imperative!* I left out, quite on purpose, what most people call spaghetti sauce, figuring that everyone had a favorite — probably based on a can of the stuff doctored up with bits of dried herbs and meats, for I've always considered spaghetti coated with cooked tomato sauce to be one of life's drearier dishes. But when a reader addressed the question of tomato sauce with perhaps a bit of *cinnamon* in it, the idea of *roasting* the ingredients surfaced, as did this King of Sauces. For it, you must go out into your own or someone else's garden and pick all the tomatoes that are mostly to very ripe. On top of them you pile other vegetables of the peak-to-end-of-summer garden that are waiting for their lives to be justified by being eaten. They may include leeks, carrots, onions, garlic, fennel, peppers of all colors, shapes, and pungency, and lovage or celery — all to be roasted. We make several batches of this over the summer, putting it over spaghetti with just a grating of Parmesan the first night, adding some red wine and chopped clams a night later, marinating Cornish game hens in it (see p. 139), and even dipping it up on corn chips for a snack. One of the nicest things about any of these suppers is that there, on the counter, 6 pints of tomato sauce linger where once there were too many tomatoes and peppers. Each batch has a slightly different taste according to the weather and the choice of vegetables included, so be sure to mark the vintage on each jar.

Makes 6 to 8 pints

10 pounds ripe tomatoes
3 large carrots with
　ferns left on
1 bulb fennel with stems
　and ferns
5 leeks, pale green and
　white parts only
2 green peppers
2 red peppers
1 head of garlic
2 stems of lovage (or
　celery)
1 large, sharp onion
2 hot peppers (jalapeño,
　New Mexican, or
　chipotle)

½ cup olive oil
2 cups inexpensive red
　wine
herbs such as parsley,
　marjoram, thyme, or
　oregano
1 tablespoon cinnamon
salt and pepper to taste
dollop of Dried Tomato
　Harissa (p. 144), or
　to taste
1 to 2 tablespoons sugar
⅓ cup cider vinegar

Slash the top of each tomato and squeeze out the seeds and water. Put a thick layer of the tomatoes in a broiler pan, filling it almost full. Scrub the carrots, fennel, and leeks, cut them into rough chunks, and place on top of the tomatoes. Quarter the green and red peppers, putting the stem end attached to the seeds into the pan along with the quarters. Separate the head of garlic into cloves and scatter them over, and add the lovage or celery. Wash the onion, cut into quarters, and add. Tuck the hot peppers into the tomatoes. Place the remaining tomatoes on top.

Place the pan in a 450-degree oven and roast for ½ hour. Open the oven and push the harder vegetables down into the softened tomatoes. Roast for another ½ hour or until the vegetables are all very soft.

Take from the oven and reduce the heat to 400 degrees. Let the vegetables cool a bit in the pan before ladling them into the bowl of the food processor. Chop them fine and pour into a food mill over a large bowl. When all the vegetables have been pureed, pour back into the roasting pan and add the olive oil, wine, herbs, cinnamon, salt and pepper, and harissa.

Stir in the sugar and the vinegar. This is a juggling act, and much of the sauce's final taste depends upon it. These are about the right amounts for the best-tasting tomatoes at peak season, which, here in Vermont, would be mid- to late August. As tomatoes are subjected to colder weather they become less sweet. Late-season tomatoes will need more sugar, up to ⅓ cup. Don't worry, the vinegar and sugar will not cancel each other out, but add to the flavor.

Return the mixture to the oven until reduced to desired consistency and flavors are melded, another ½ hour. Ladle into sterilized jars and process in a boiling water bath for 40 minutes.

Golden Tomato Sauce for Pasta

Robust and savory, this sauce is mellowed in both color and flavor by the golden tomatoes and sweetened with the peppers. Spoon it over ziti or penne to funnel it up. If pancetta — unsmoked Italian bacon — is unavailable, use prosciutto or sidepork (an unsmoked bacon).

Serves 4

2 tablespoons olive oil	1 tablespoon fresh,
¼ pound pancetta, cut in	shredded sage leaves
thin strips	½ teaspoon salt
1 cup sliced onion	¼ teaspoon freshly
2 cups sliced yellow	ground pepper
pepper	½ pound ziti or penne
4 cups yellow tomato	pasta
crescents	freshly grated Parmesan

Heat oil in a large skillet over medium heat and sauté pancetta for several minutes, until it begins to color slightly. Stir in onion and continue to cook for 5 minutes or until it is wilted, then add the yellow pepper, tomatoes, sage, salt, and pepper, stirring well. Cover and cook over medium-low heat for 20 minutes or until thick.

Meanwhile, cook pasta in a large pot of boiling salted water until al dente. Drain well, toss with the sauce, and pass the cheese.

Five Stuffed Tomatoes and One Zucchini

François's Ricotta-Stuffed Plum Tomatoes

A cool, quick, tasty appetizer or party offering when made with garden-fresh tomatoes and herbs and the best ricotta. From Ruth's friend François Dinand. Stuffing plum tomatoes is far less fussy than stuffing cherry tomatoes.

Serves 12 as an appetizer

12 ripe plum tomatoes, cored, halved, and seeded
1 tablespoon kosher salt
1 cup ricotta
½ cup sour cream
½ teaspoon salt
¼ teaspoon freshly ground pepper

1 garlic clove, minced
1 tablespoon each minced parsley and basil
1 tablespoon snipped chives

Sprinkle the tomatoes with kosher salt and turn upside down to drain for 1 hour. Mix remaining ingredients together and spoon into tomato halves. Sprinkle with chopped chives. Serve on summer greens.

Perfectly Poached Chicken and Broth

This easy method makes the best chicken for salad and a light broth (see below).

Yields 3 cups of cut-up chicken

1 3½-pound whole chicken, giblets removed and reserved
3 quarts water
1 unpeeled onion, halved, or two scallions
1 stalk celery
1 piece of fresh gingerroot the size of a quarter

Bring water and vegetables to a boil in a large pot over high heat. Put the chicken into the pot. When the water returns to a boil, cover, remove from heat, and let stand 1 hour. The chicken can then be removed from the liquid (reserve it), skinned, boned, and cut up.

Tomatoes Stuffed with Circassian Chicken Salad

This sumptuous dish is named for a cold walnut dressing that hails from the Caucasus mountain region of Georgia, where the Circassian walnut grows. This is a variation on a recipe given Ruth by a friend long ago.

Serves 4

½ cup hazelnuts
4 large ripe tomatoes (8 ounces apiece)
kosher salt
2 cups diced Perfectly Poached Chicken
½ cup toasted walnuts
2 tablespoons minced fresh parsley
2 tablespoons minced fresh cilantro
½ teaspoon minced garlic
2 tablespoons red wine vinegar
¾ teaspoon kosher salt
⅛ teaspoon freshly ground pepper
⅛ teaspoon cayenne
6 tablespoons olive oil
2 bunches of watercress

Toast the hazelnuts in a 350-degree oven for 10 minutes. Take them from the oven and put them in a dish towel. Rub the skins off the hazelnuts with the towel. Set aside.

Cut off the top half inch of each tomato. With a small knife cut around the inside of the tomato wall and scoop out the seeds and pulp with your finger. Sprinkle with kosher salt and drain upside down for 1 hour.

Toss the chicken with the nuts and herbs in a bowl. In another bowl whisk the vinegar with salt, pepper, and cayenne. Whisk in the oil until well blended and toss with chicken mixture. Mound the chicken in the tomato shells in a dish, cover, and chill for several hours to let the flavors mellow and mingle.

Serve on a bed of watercress.

Tomatoes Stuffed with Pasta, Tuna, and Black Olives

Ruth likes to use the dark, flavorful, and moist Progresso brand tuna, packed in olive oil. Others like to use a chunk white tuna packed in water, in which case add a bit of olive oil to it. Please use imported pasta, such as DeCecco, which will keep its firm texture when stuffed in the tomato.

Serves 4

4 large tomatoes
kosher salt
7 ounces cooked pasta
 — small elbow,
 ditalini, or small ziti
1 9-ounce can tuna (see
 above), drained and
 flaked
3 medium tomatoes
 (¾ pound), peeled,
 seeded, and chopped
12 oil-cured black
 olives, pitted and
 chopped

⅔ cup Basic Mayonnaise
 (p. 66)
8 anchovy fillets,
 chopped
3 tablespoons capers
¼ teaspoon freshly
 ground pepper or
 more to taste
2 tablespoons minced
 fresh basil
1½ tablespoons lemon
 juice
basil leaves

Light Chicken Broth

The bones and reserved giblets (all but the liver, which you feed to the cat) can be returned to the pot with the poaching liquid and simmered for 2½ hours to make a broth.

Rich Chicken Broth

Cover a cut-up chicken with cold water, bring to a simmer, and, never boiling, cook gently for 2½ hours. The chicken itself will have given most of its flavor to the delicious broth but can still be used for an old-fashioned chicken pot pie or any chicken-and-gravy type of dish.

Cut off the top half inch of each large tomato. With a small knife cut around the inside of the tomato wall and scoop out seeds and pulp with your finger. Sprinkle with kosher salt and drain upside down for at least 20 minutes, preferably an hour.

Toss remaining ingredients together and fill the drained tomatoes. Tuck a large basil leaf in each tomato for a garnish.

An Egg Baked in a Tomato

Simplicity itself, and perfect, but you must monitor carefully, as ovens and altitudes are highly subjective. Once you've got it down, this method can be a convenient way of serving many eggs at one time. Serve with Bruschetta (p. 90) or buttered toast, or atop pasta tossed with olive oil and Parmesan, for breakfast, lunch, or an intriguing midnight snack.

Serves 2

2 medium meaty, ripe tomatoes	coarse salt
	freshly ground pepper
2 teaspoons fruity olive oil	chopped parsley
	grated Parmesan
2 large eggs	(optional)

Heat oven to 400 degrees. Slice off the top third of each tomato. Hook out the seeds with your little finger, but do not damage the structure. Put each tomato into a small ramekin that has been very lightly oiled and put them in the oven for 10 minutes or until hot. When the tomatoes are just beginning to cook, take them from the oven, break an egg into each, sprinkle each egg with salt and pepper to taste, parsley, the rest of the olive oil, and then the Parmesan, if you please. Replace in the oven and bake 5 to 7 minutes or until the eggs are just set. The yolks won't color, so be sure not to overbake them. Serve immediately.

Persian Rice Baked in Tomatoes

As good cold as hot, as good the next day as on the day you make it, this is a simple luncheon full of exotic flavors. The brown rice is nutty, and the almonds add crunch. Ruth likes the texture and flavor that nuts add to dishes, and she uses them in creative ways. They are particularly suitable to vegetarian dishes. Brown basmati rice can be found at your local health food store and some supermarkets. It must be cooked longer than white — about 35 to 40 minutes.

Serves 4

4 large, ripe, firm tomatoes (8 ounces each)	2 tablespoons minced fresh parsley
½ tablespoon kosher salt	½ teaspoon salt
1½ cups cooked brown rice (preferably brown basmati)	¼ teaspoon ground cardamom
½ cup toasted almonds, very coarsely chopped	¼ teaspoon freshly ground pepper
¼ cup currants	1 tablespoon lemon juice
2 tablespoons minced fresh cilantro	3 tablespoons melted butter

Cut off the top half inch of each tomato. With a small knife cut around the inside of the tomato wall and scoop out seeds and pulp with your finger. Sprinkle with kosher salt and drain upside down for 20 minutes to an hour.

Preheat oven to 350 degrees.

Mix rice with almonds, currants, cilantro, parsley, salt, cardamom, and pepper. Butter a shallow 8-inch round baking dish that holds the tomatoes snugly and fill them with the rice mixture. Mix the lemon juice with the melted butter and drizzle over the tops of the tomatoes.

Add ¼ inch of water to the pan and bake for 35 minutes. Don't overbake as the tomatoes will collapse.

Zucchini Stuffed with Sausage and Sauce

There is no shortage of jokes about careless Vermonters who leave their car doors unlocked during zucchini season, only to return and find the car overflowing with zucchini, so prolific are these plants. Remember, two hills of zucchini in the garden will keep you and your neighbors well supplied with blossoms to stuff and fry as well as with the vegetable itself, and this is a classic way to treat them. A melon baller is a great little tool for lots more jobs than its name suggests; it can core a halved pear, as well as seed a zucchini or a cucumber neatly and succinctly.

Serves 4 to 6 as a main dish

4 zucchinis, each
    6 inches long, halved
    lengthwise
½ pound hot Italian
    sausage
1 cup finely chopped
    onion
3 cups coarsely chopped
    ripe tomatoes

½ teaspoon salt
⅛ teaspoon freshly
    ground pepper
Roasted Tomato and
    Vegetable Sauce
    (p. 110)

Using a teaspoon or melon baller, scoop out zucchini pulp, leaving a ⅓-inch shell. Chop the pulp fine and set aside.

Remove casing from the sausage, crumble the meat into a large skillet over medium heat, and brown. Stir in the chopped zucchini pulp, onion, tomatoes, salt, and pepper, and cook over medium-low heat until the mixture is thick, about 15 to 20 minutes.

Preheat oven to 350 degrees. Place zucchini halves in a large baking pan (a lasagna pan works nicely) and mound with equal amounts of the meat mixture. Pour ¼ inch of hot water around the zucchini, cover the pan loosely with foil, and bake for about 30 minutes or until the zucchini is just tender. Do not overbake.

Serve each zucchini half in a pool of warm Roasted Tomato and Vegetable Sauce on individual plates.

Soups

High Summer Soup

*Y*OU'LL find the makings of this soup in your garden on a hot August day. All the vegetable flavors come together in cream-of-the-garden with no reliance on meat broth. Be sure to soak the cauliflower in salt water to get the little green critters out. You can make the soup in high winter, too, and then you don't have to soak, but of course you won't have the same ultra-fresh flavor. I like the slight Middle Eastern flavorings the Dried Tomato Harissa gives, but if you haven't made it from our recipe on p. 144, you can substitute a small hot pepper and half a teaspoon each of cumin and coriander, ground. Adding the beurre manié brings all the ingredients together in a smooth unity.

Serves 4

1 large head of
  cauliflower, trimmed
  and separated into
  florets
2 tablespoons unsalted
  butter
3 large leeks, whites and
  pale greens, cleaned
  well and chopped
1 large fennel bulb,
  trimmed and cut into
  crescents
1 large stem of lovage,
  chopped (or
  substitute celery)
6 large tomatoes, cored
  and quartered

1 teaspoon sugar
1 to 2 tablespoons Dried
  Tomato Harissa or to
  taste
coarse salt
freshly ground pepper
1 teaspoon flour mashed
  with 1 teaspoon
  butter (beurre manié)
approximately 1 cup
  whole milk
chopped leaves of lovage
  and tender fennel
  ferns
Bruschetta (p. 90)

In a large bowl soak the cauliflower for at least half an hour in heavily salted cold water to cover. In a large, deep sauté pan melt the butter over medium heat, then add the leeks, fennel, and lovage, and lower the heat. Rinse cauliflower and add it to the pan. Simmer until cauliflower is becoming tender, add the tomatoes, crunching them into pieces, and add the sugar. When everything is tender and the tomatoes have given off their juice, about 20 minutes, take from the heat and let cool a few minutes. If you like, chop the vegetables briefly in the bowl of a food processor before putting through a food mill. Pour back into the sauté pan and add the harissa and salt and pepper to taste. Whisk bits of the beurre manié into the soup until it becomes satiny. Stir in the milk, heat just to serving temperature, correct seasonings, and serve with a sprinkling of chopped lovage and fennel ferns, with Bruschetta on the side.

Labor Day Roasted Lobster Chowder

When the corn comes popping out of its husks, which is perhaps not so coincidentally the time when Maine lobsters are available in considerable number and at a decent price, it's time to pull out a tattered recipe for corn and lobster chowder, in which the lobster and corn and other vegetables are first grilled, then the gutted shells and broken cobs are covered with fresh water and simmered together with seasonings for a little over an hour. When this broth is strained, it is the essence of corn and lobster; and when this essence is added to the grilled sausage, onion, potatoes, corn, and cooked lobster, along with cream, it is ambrosial. The technique of making the broth comes from Boston restaurateur Jasper White, than whom no one is better at hoarding and highlighting seafood and other flavors. We adapted that to our own technique of grilling the ingredients and *voilà* — a wonderful smoky-flavored stew, thick and fresh. Leaving the root ends on the onions and leeks even when quartering them lengthwise keeps the segments together when grilling them. A bit of hickory that has been soaked for half an hour in water does not detract from the final flavor, but don't use too much. Tuck it down in among the coals when they are white. Adding the ripest, freshest tomatoes at the end simply highlights all of the creamy, rich flavors of seafood and cream.

Serves 6

3 ears of corn with husks on	2 tablespoons butter
2 fat leeks, quartered lengthwise through root end	1 tablespoon minced fresh thyme leaves
1 large Spanish onion, unpeeled, quartered through root end	1 pound small new potatoes, scrubbed and cut in ½-inch chunks
½ pound chorizo sausage	4 large tomatoes, peeled, seeded, and chopped (2½ cups)
1 jalapeño pepper or chipotle	1 cup light cream
3 pounds live lobsters (2 or 3)	salt and pepper to taste
1 bay leaf	chopped parsley

Soak the corn clothed in its husks in a pail of cold water for half an hour, while you heat the grill very hot. If the grill does not have a cover, make one out of heavy aluminum foil.

Wash and trim the tough green leek tops and put them in a broth pot big enough to hold the corncobs and the lobster carcasses as well. Do not trim the roots of the leeks and the onion, but rinse the quartered leeks well to get rid of the dirt between the layers. Set aside.

When the grill is hot, drain the corn and throw it on the grill. Thread the leeks, onion, sausage, and jalapeño on two long skewers if they would be in danger of falling through the grill, and place on a cooler area of the grill. Cover and roast 10 minutes, turning everything, checking to see that nothing is charring too badly. Keep turning the ears of corn, the husks of which will blacken while the kernels inside are caramelizing. Remove the leeks, onion, sausage, and jalapeños.

Push the corn to the edge of the grill and throw the lobsters on the grill, cover, and let them roast 7 or 8 minutes, until they are bright red. Remove the lobsters and corn and set aside in a pan large enough to catch any juices until they are cool enough to handle.

Husk the corn and slice the kernels into a bowl, retaining any juices. Cut the cobs in pieces and put them in the broth pot with the leek tops. Add the bay leaf. Break off the lobster claws and tail and extract the meat, using a nutcracker on the claws and pushing the tail meat out with your fingers. Pick out any other meat from arms and body — a child is good at this. Save the red coral the hens may have and leave the green tomalley with the carcasses. Cut meat into bite-sized chunks and refrigerate with the coral.

Put the carcasses in the pot with the corncobs and squash down as much as possible. Cover with 2 quarts of cold fresh water, bring to a boil, turn the heat to medium low, cover, and simmer for 1 hour. Strain, reserving the broth. You should have almost 8 cups of good broth. Freeze any that you don't use.

Meanwhile, melt the butter in a large soup pot over low heat. Dice the sausage and chop the grilled leeks and onion, discarding the roots, and add to the pot. Slit the jalapeño, discard seeds, mince, and add to the pot along with the thyme leaves and potatoes. Stir to coat the vegetables with the butter, cover, and cook 10 minutes over medium heat, then add 1 cup of broth and cook 5 minutes more or until potatoes are tender. Add the tomatoes, reserved corn, 3 cups of broth, cream, and salt and pepper to taste. Bring to a simmer, turn the heat to low, add the lobster meat, and simmer just until the lobster is warmed through. Add more broth, if needed. Correct the seasoning. Serve sprinkled with parsley.

Vegetable and Side Dishes

Tabbouleh

*T*HERE is not a much better thing in the world than a well-made salad of crisp, dark green parsley, with chunks of ripe tomato and hearty, chewy grains, all dressed with the juice of a lemon. Ours combines three grains — the addition of nuts brings out the nuttiness of the grains.

Serves 6

⅓ cup coarse cracked wheat (bulgur) soaked in 2 cups of water for 1 hour
⅓ cup short-grain brown rice
⅓ cup barley
3 cups diced tomatoes (1½ pounds)
1 cup peeled, diced cucumber
5 chopped scallions

½ cup minced Italian parsley
¼ cup minced mint
⅓ cup toasted, chopped almonds and/or hazelnuts
¼ cup lemon juice
½ cup olive oil
1 teaspoon salt
¼ teaspoon cinnamon
¼ teaspoon freshly ground pepper

Cook the rice and barley together in a pot of boiling salted water for 25 minutes or until the grains are tender but al dente. Drain and rinse in cold water, drain again, and place in a large bowl. Drain the cracked wheat very well and add it to the bowl. Add the tomatoes, cucumber, scallions, herbs, and nuts to the bowl.

In a small bowl whisk together the lemon juice, olive oil, salt, cinnamon, and pepper. Add to the grains, taste for seasoning, and chill for several hours.

Baked Ratatouille with Lemon Basil Crumbs

Ruth prepares this as a buffet dish for large summer gatherings or potluck suppers, to be served hot or at room temperature. Both of its components can be made a day ahead of time and then assembled on the serving day. People always ask for the recipe. Now they'll ask you.

Serves 10 to 12

2 pounds eggplant cut in
   1-inch cubes (9 cups)
2 tablespoons kosher
   salt
3 tablespoons olive oil
2 large onions, halved
   lengthwise and sliced
1 teaspoon minced
   garlic
1 pound green peppers,
   seeded and cut in
   strips (3½ cups)
1 pound zucchini, cubed
   (3 cups)

1 large fennel bulb,
   coarsely chopped
   (2 cups)
4 large tomatoes (2
   pounds), cored and
   quartered
2 tablespoons minced
   fresh basil
2 tablespoons minced
   fresh parsley
½ teaspoon salt
¼ teaspoon freshly
   ground pepper

Crumb topping:

1 teaspoon minced
   garlic
1 tablespoon minced
   fresh basil
1 tablespoon minced
   fresh parsley
1 cup dry or toasted
   bread crumbs

½ cup freshly grated
   Parmesan cheese
grated rind of 1 large
   lemon
3 tablespoons olive oil
¼ teaspoon salt
⅛ teaspoon freshly
   ground pepper

Place the eggplant cubes in a large bowl and toss liberally with kosher salt, then put into a colander and allow to drain for half an hour. Squeeze by handfuls to remove excess water.

Heat oil in a large ovenproof skillet over medium-high heat and brown the eggplant for several minutes, stirring. Add the onions and garlic and continue to cook, stirring occasionally, for about 5 minutes. Stir in peppers, zucchini, and fennel and cook 5 minutes longer. Add tomatoes, herbs, salt, and pepper, toss, and cover. Lower heat and simmer the mixture for about ½ hour. Spoon the vegetables into a 3-quart gratin dish or shallow baking dish, and preheat oven to 400 degrees.

In a bowl toss garlic, basil, parsley, crumbs, cheese, and lemon rind together. Drizzle with olive oil, sprinkle with salt and freshly ground pepper, and toss. Correct seasonings.

Sprinkle the crumb topping evenly over the vegetable mixture and bake ½ hour on the top shelf of the oven, until crumbs are golden brown.

Sauté of Okra and Tomatoes with Ginger

Okra is a gorgeous plant, tall and green with a flower like a beautiful hibiscus, and I've had good luck with it in my northern garden, although it does like a bit of heat. The okra pod itself is wonderful pickled, grilled, or fried, or sautéed quickly as Ruth does it here, nicely gingered. When you buy gingerroot, just break off as much of the knob as you can use in the foreseeable future. It lasts quite a long time at room temperature, although it continues to dry. It can also be wrapped in plastic and frozen. Ruth peels a whole gingerroot, cuts it into pieces to fit into a glass jar, then covers it with rice wine or sherry or gin or vodka, and refrigerates it. Take out what you need when you need it, but no sipping!

Serves 4 to 6

2 tablespoons vegetable oil	1 pound small, fresh okra, whole (if you use frozen, don't thaw it)
1 tablespoon minced garlic	
2 tablespoons pared and minced gingerroot	½ teaspoon salt
3 large tomatoes, chopped (3 cups)	⅛ teaspoon freshly ground pepper
¼ teaspoon crushed hot red pepper	

Heat oil in a large skillet over medium heat and add the garlic, ginger, tomatoes, and red pepper. Cook for 2 minutes, stirring. Add okra and salt and pepper, stir well, cover, and cook 10 to 15 minutes until the okra is just tender.

Anna's Green Beans and Potatoes

We're partial to this recipe for more reasons than that it is delicious. It came to us via Ruth's sister-in-law's mother's mother, Anna Riccio Jacobs, and it was handed down from one cook to the next, until here it is — a classic hearty southern Italian dish, toothsome served hot or cold. Make it with peak summer tomatoes and take it on a picnic, or use a 28-ounce can of tomatoes on a blizzardy day in January and just pretend you're going on a picnic. We prefer waxy red potatoes in this, although you can use russets if you keep in mind that they are more likely to fall apart, thereby thickening the sauce. If you have leftovers, add some browned sweet or hot Italian sausage, and simmer 15 minutes to blend flavors.

Serves 6 to 8

3 large ripe tomatoes, chopped (3 cups)
2 tablespoons olive oil
2 tablespoons minced garlic
1 pound string beans, trimmed and cut into 2-inch lengths

2½ pounds potatoes, peeled and cut in 1-inch cubes (about 5½ cups)
1 tablespoon salt
¼ teaspoon freshly ground pepper

Put tomatoes through a food mill to remove skins and seeds. Heat the oil in a large pot over medium heat and add tomatoes and remaining ingredients. Bring to a simmer, cover, and cook until vegetables are tender, about 25 to 30 minutes.

Anchovied Potatoes with Tomatoes and Onions

A wonderful accompaniment to roast meats — good cold, delicious hot.

Serves 6 to 8

4 tablespoons fruity virgin olive oil	2 pounds firm, slightly waxy potatoes (Yukon Gold are good),
3 cups sliced onion	
12 chopped anchovy fillets	peeled and very thinly sliced
1 pound tomatoes (2 medium), peeled and thinly sliced	¾ teaspoon salt
	freshly ground pepper

Preheat oven to 350 degrees. Heat 2 tablespoons of the olive oil in a skillet over medium heat and stir in onion and anchovies. Cover and cook slowly until onion is wilted, about 10 minutes. Oil a shallow gratin dish with 1 tablespoon of the oil, then alternate layers of the onion mixture, tomatoes, and potatoes, sprinkling potato layers with salt and pepper. Finally, drizzle the remaining tablespoon of oil over the top. Cover with foil and bake for 1 hour 40 minutes, until the potatoes are very tender.

Tomato Fennel Risotto

"What is that flavor?" my son, Spencer, exclaimed the first time I stirred fennel, lovage, and tomato into a risotto. There should be a name for the single resonant flavor that results when these are combined. Stirring the rice and broth together almost constantly is what makes this dish so creamy.

Serves 6 to 8

4½ cups Rich Chicken
    Broth (p. 116)
1 tablespoon butter
2 tablespoons light olive
    oil
1 cup chopped onion
1 large fennel bulb,
    including tender
    stalks, coarsely
    chopped (3 cups)
1 stalk of lovage (or
    celery with leaves)

1 cup arborio rice
1 pound ripe tomatoes
    (2 medium), peeled,
    seeded, and chopped
1 teaspoon salt
⅛ teaspoon freshly
    ground pepper
½ cup freshly grated
    Parmesan cheese
1 tablespoon finely
    chopped fennel ferns

Heat Chicken Broth and hold at a simmer.

Heat butter and oil in a large skillet over medium-high heat. Sauté onion, fennel, and lovage until golden, about 10 minutes. Add rice and stir for 1 minute to coat grains with oil. Lower heat to medium low and add broth a ladleful (¼ cup) at a time, stirring frequently, letting the rice absorb the liquid before adding the next ladleful. When the rice is al dente, add in the tomatoes, salt, pepper, and the rest of the broth, and stir another few minutes until the sauce is creamy.

Take from heat, stir in cheese, sprinkle with chopped greens, and serve immediately.

Eggplant Pie

The idea for this dish came to us from an old sixties-style health-food recipe. It had a fine taste but was terribly gray, an unattractive mass. We separated the elements to make a delicious and beautiful dish. If you can't find fontina, use another creamy cheese — Emmentaler or Gruyère would do nicely. Be sure to start this early to salt the eggplant.

Serves 6 to 8 as a first course or side dish, 4 to 6 as a main dish

2 medium-sized
   eggplants
coarse salt
2 tablespoons olive oil
3 large ripe tomatoes
   (1½ pounds)
12 ounces fontina
   cheese, grated
1 small bunch of basil
   (20 leaves)
3 large eggs, lightly
   beaten
2 tablespoons melted
   butter

3 tablespoons chopped
   onion
½ cup dry Bread Crumbs
   (p. 90)
1 teaspoon salt
½ teaspoon freshly
   ground pepper
1 tablespoon oil for the
   pan
1 pint Roasted Tomato
   and Vegetable Sauce
   (p. 110)

At least 2 hours before serving time, trim off the ends of the eggplants and discard. Slice the eggplants lengthwise in thin (¼-inch), unpared slices. A glossy purple skin will make a nicer finished pattern. Salt the slices heavily and allow to drain for at least half an hour in a colander. In the meantime, skin, core, halve, and seed the tomatoes, then slice them ⅓ inch thick.

Rinse salt off the eggplant and pat dry with a kitchen towel. Brush with oil and grill or broil until just tender.

Preheat oven to 375 degrees. Oil an 8½-inch or 9-inch deep-dish pie plate. If possible, the sides should be vertical and at least 1½ inches high. Place the narrower end of an eggplant slice in the middle of the bottom of the dish. Shape it up the side and allow it to hang over the edge. Lap the next slice slightly over the first, and continue until you have a spiral of eggplant slices completely lining the dish. Patch any gaps. You'll have several slices left.

Scatter half the grated cheese over the eggplant. Cover the cheese with a layer of tomato slices. Tear the basil leaves over the tomatoes and add another layer of tomatoes. Sprinkle lightly with salt and pepper.

Mix eggs, butter, onion, Bread Crumbs, and salt and pepper and spread over the tomatoes. Top with the remaining cheese, place two or three of the remaining eggplant slices over the pie, and bring the overlapping pieces up to seal. Bake for 30 to 45 minutes at 375 degrees.

Let the pie rest for 5 minutes, then invert the baking dish over a serving platter. Let it rest upside down for a few minutes, then carefully lift the baking dish and ease any stuck parts out with a spatula. Warm the Roasted Tomato and Vegetable Sauce over medium heat. If serving the pie whole, spoon the sauce around it and serve. If serving it by the plate, spoon a pool of tomato sauce onto each plate and then place a wedge of the pie in the sauce.

Biscuit Pie Like Grandma's

As we browsed through old books and community cookbooks, we began to notice a tomato pie — nothing more than biscuit dough pressed into a pie pan, covered with sliced tomatoes, sprinkled with cheddar cheese, and topped with a mixture of mayonnaise, onion, and parsley before being baked. Laurie Colwin wrote of one she had found in a Connecticut tea shop, with a double, buttery biscuit crust, which had also originally come from a community cookbook. We made one by a recipe that had been submitted by Betty Stewart of Pittsford and was included in the *Vermont Symphony Cookbook,* one of our favorite books of this genre. Ours here is luscious in a way we didn't expect. It uses a single crust, but you could double the biscuit and put on a top crust, no problem.

Serves 4 to 6

1 cup flour
2 teaspoons baking powder
½ teaspoon salt
¼ cup unsalted butter
approximately ⅓ cup whole milk
4 ripe tomatoes (2 pounds), thickly sliced

1 tablespoon chopped fresh thyme leaves
1¼ cups shredded sharp cheddar cheese
1 double shallot, minced
1 garlic clove, smashed, peeled, and minced
⅓ cup mayonnaise
3 tablespoons minced parsley

Preheat oven to 375 degrees. Make the biscuit by combining the flour and baking powder in a bowl, cut in the butter until texture is crumbly, then add milk until the dough comes together. The dough will be a trifle wet. Flour it well and roll and pat it out to fit a 9-inch deep-dish pie plate. Layer in the tomatoes, sprinkle the fresh thyme over the tomatoes, and strew with 1 cup of the cheese. Mix the shallot and garlic in the mayonnaise and spread the mixture over the cheese. Top with remaining ¼ cup of cheese, sprinkle with the parsley, and bake for 45 minutes or until the biscuit is done. Serve it hot. Any leftovers must be reheated until the cheese is melted again.

Tomato and Mozzarella Tart Al Ducci's

In the town of Manchester in Vermont is a great little Italian grocery called Al Ducci's, where owner Al Shep makes mozzarella the way it should be made — fresh every day. He also makes creamy fresh ricotta and a chewy, close-grained semolina bread daily. He gave me this method for the very rich tart he sells there by the piece, which utilizes his own mozzarella, of course.

Serves 6 as a first course

1 recipe Italian Butter Pastry (p. 35), chilled for 1 hour

2 rounded tablespoons grainy country mustard

1 pound fresh wholemilk mozzarella cheese, sliced thin

5 medium, ripe tomatoes, cored and sliced thin

3 garlic cloves, smashed, peeled, and finely chopped

coarse salt

freshly ground pepper

2 tablespoons fresh oregano leaves, or 2 teaspoons dried

3 tablespoons extra-virgin olive oil

Preheat oven to 400 degrees. Roll out the Italian Butter Pastry and fit it into a 10-inch tart pan with a removable bottom. Brush the pastry with the mustard and overlap slices of mozzarella to cover it completely. Then overlap the tomato slices to cover the cheese completely. Sprinkle with the garlic, salt and pepper to taste, and oregano. Drizzle with olive oil and bake about 45 minutes, or until the cheese is melted, the tomatoes are tender, the whole is bubbling, and the aroma compels you to take it out and eat it. Force yourself to wait a few minutes until it cools a bit.

Main Dishes from the Grill

Mixed Vegetable Grill with Lamb

S ERVE this peak-of-summer salad alone or with thin pink slices of a lamb part that has been grilled over a bit of hickory. We keep a small shaker bottle filled with good olive oil in which a couple of cloves of garlic steep permanently (refrigerated), in which case we can skip the first instruction. We find fresh chanterelle mushrooms in nearby woods during July and August, and sometimes they can be found at the market.

You may serve this as a layered salad: cold fresh greens on the bottom, warm grilled vegetables in the middle, the sizzling-hot grilled lamb on top — the whole garlicky, lemony, and positively Mediterranean. It makes a great sandwich the next day.

Serves 4 to 6

½ cup good, fruity olive
  oil
4 garlic cloves, smashed
  and peeled
2½ pounds boneless
  lamb (a partial leg
  will do)
1 medium eggplant
coarse salt
1 large sweet onion
2 fat leeks
6 small okra pods
1 meaty red pepper
2 small yellow summer
  squash, cut in 1-inch
  diagonal rounds

3 ripe tomatoes, halved
12 whole fresh
  chanterelles or other
  wild mushrooms such
  as shiitake
1 small bunch of basil
3 lemons
freshly ground black
  pepper
1 quart mixed salad
  greens, washed and
  chilled

One hour before grilling, mince 2 of the cloves of garlic and steep in the oil. With a small knife make gashes in the lamb, sliver the remaining 2 cloves of garlic, and push the slivers into the gashes. Set the lamb aside. Slice the eggplant in ½-inch slices, dip each side of each slice in coarse salt, and put in a colander to drain.

Start the coals in a covered grill. Peel the onion, leaving the bristly root end alone, then quarter vertically so that the root end holds each segment together. String on a skewer. Do not trim the roots of the leeks. Trim dark green leaves and quarter vertically to within ½ inch of the root. Spread the quarters apart, wash, and trim to remove any sand. Leave the okra whole. Trim the stem ends of the mushrooms, brushing off any debris. Rinse the eggplant of salt and pat dry. Arrange all the ingredients on a large tray, along with utensils.

When the coals are ready, roast the lamb on the grill, covered, for 30 minutes. Raise the cover and continue to roast the lamb for another 15 minutes, while you roast the vegetables.

Roast the whole pepper, turning it until the skin is charred. Remove to a plate and fling a towel over to steam it a bit until the skin peels off easily (see p. 15). Sliver the pepper and put it, with any juices, in a large crockery bowl. Sprinkle the squash and other vegetables with some of the garlic oil and grill: the eggplant should be grilled on both sides until puddinglike inside and browned outside. The skewered onion should be turned often, and the tomato halves should be grilled on a cooler part of the grill until they begin to collapse. Grill the okra and chanterelles whole, and the leeks spread like flowers.

Remove the lamb to a cutting board and allow to rest for 10 minutes.

Add each vegetable piece to the bowl as it is ready, breaking the eggplant and tomatoes into several pieces as you do so. Trim off the root ends of the onion and leeks so segments separate. Tear the basil leaves over all. Toss with the juice of 1 or 2 lemons and as much of the garlic oil as you like. Correct the seasonings.

In a large glass salad bowl toss the cold greens with the juice of 1 lemon and garlic oil to taste. Mound the warm grilled vegetables over the greens. Place thin slices of hot lamb over all and serve. Alternatively, arrange the three courses separately and attractively on a large platter and serve immediately.

Roasted and Grilled Cornish Game Hens

"Spatchcocking" is an old English term for removing the backbone of a chicken or other fowl in order to flatten it for grilling and oven-roasting, allowing for more even cooking and very easy serving. We prefer to prebake the about-to-be grilled bird so as to eliminate the problem of raw inside and burned outside, which happens all too often in grilling. In this recipe marinating overnight allows the flavor of the sauce to penetrate the flesh.

Serves 4 but can be multiplied

2 Cornish game hens, **¼ cup malt, sherry, or**
 approximately **balsamic vinegar**
 1¼ pounds each **1 tablespoon honey**
1 cup Roasted Tomato coarse salt
 and Vegetable Sauce
 (p. 110)

Remove the giblets from the hens' cavities and freeze for soup. Using a sharp knife, cut down from behind and through the thigh joint, down along the ribs, staying close to the backbone and finishing by cutting through the wing joint. Repeat on the other side. Now the hens can be spread flat out, skin side up. Make a small slash through the loose skin under the leg and insert the end of the leg in it. Do this on both sides. This holds the legs neatly in place during cooking. Finally, tuck the wing tips under the top of the breasts. Place hens in a noncorrosive pan. Combine the Roasted Tomato and Vegetable Sauce, vinegar, and honey and pour over hens. Cover and refrigerate overnight, turning the hens several times in the marinade.

Remove hens from the refrigerator an hour before grilling. Heat the oven to 350 degrees. Remove the hens from the marinade and place them in a baking pan. Sprinkle both sides with salt, and bake for 40 minutes. Meanwhile, heat the grill, and when the hens are ready, grill them about 15 minutes, turning them several times and brushing them with the marinade. To serve, cut down the breastbone of each hen to separate into 2 halves.

If you wish to use the leftover marinade as a sauce, you must bring it to a boil and simmer for 20 minutes before using.

Hickory Grilled Pork Loin with Two Tastes

I own a small hoard of hickory pieces that my cousin gave me when he cut down a hickory tree. These are chunks about 6 inches by 2 inches, and I value them with my life. I soak one every once in a while to tuck into hot coals over which to grill a piece of fresh pork or a chicken, but you can buy more or less potent hickory chips commercially. Figure on ⅓ to ½ pound of meat per person.

Serves 6 to 8

¼ cup chopped flat-leaf parsley	3½ to 5 pounds loin of pork
3 stems of thyme	Roasted Green Tomato
3 tablespoons coarse salt	Salsa (p. 28)
3 garlic cloves, smashed, peeled, and chopped	Triple Red Chutney (p. 154)
olive oil	

Start the coals. Put a piece of hickory to soak. In a mortar with a pestle pound the parsley, thyme leaves stripped from the stems, salt, and garlic. Add enough olive oil to make a paste. Slash the loin of pork deeply all over with a sharp-bladed knife, and with a small spoon (I use a long-handled baby spoon) force the herb and garlic mixture deep into the slashes. Rub any extra paste over the outside of the roast and grill it, covered, in a hot grill until juices run clear — about 20 minutes per pound. Let it sit for ½ hour at least before slicing it thin and serving those thin slices with spoonfuls of each condiment.

Preserving Tomatoes

Vermont Oven-Dried Tomatoes

$\mathcal{D}$RYING tomatoes — so trendy in these times that we think of them as a new product — is simply another age-old preserving technique. It is not a new way even in the United States, where Sarah Rutledge, in *The Carolina Housewife* published in 1847, recommends, in order "To Keep Tomatoes The Whole Year," taking ripe tomatoes, skinning them, then boiling them well in a little sugar or salt until they are a paste. Then "spread them in cakes about an inch thick, and place the cakes in the sun." In three or four days they are "sufficiently dried to pack away in bags, which should hang in a dry place." She also recommends slab-drying an Italian tomato paste, which contains, as well as tomatoes, celery, carrots, onions, salt, peppers, cloves, and cinnamon.

The technique of drying works particularly well in dry lands where the sun is hot, of course, and it is common in Italy to end the season by hanging vines of cherry tomatoes to dry off the eaves of roofs. Common practice, too, is to take the larger tomatoes onto the roof, as explained in picturesque detail by Patience Gray, splitting them, sprinkling with salt, and hanging them on special racks to dry in the strong Mediterranean sun. And this in June!

Toward the end of the season here in Vermont — sometime in the middle of August — we take a half bushel of plum tomatoes, or other meaty, thick tomatoes grown especially for drying, to dry in the oven. Oven-drying is more sensible in damper climates like ours, where the sun cannot be counted on to shine. Seventeen pounds of field tomatoes equal 1 pound dried, which is a lot. We like ours moister than commercially prepared ones. In fact, we dislike most commercially prepared ones, and that's why we make our own.

To dry tomatoes, slice meaty plum tomatoes almost in half lengthwise and gently squeeze out seeds and juice. You may sprinkle with coarse salt, although we don't, usually. Arrange them on racks that will fit in your oven, over pans or strips of foil to catch the juices, in an oven turned to lowest heat if it is electric. Sufficient heat will probably be provided by the pilot light if your oven is a gas one. Prop open the oven door just slightly with the handle of a wooden spoon, to allow the moisture to escape the oven. After they have been in the oven for several hours — I think this takes about 16 hours, depending on initial moisture content — begin to rotate them and sort through for dried ones. They should feel leathery rather than brittle. If they are very dry, they will keep with no further preparation, but if you leave them with more moisture intact, then layer them with herbs, such as mint, marjoram, thyme, or oregano, in small jars, cover with olive oil, and refrigerate. If you must use the oven in the meantime, you can remove the racks of tomatoes for a short time. Simply resume drying when the oven has cooled again.

Eat them over the winter as a snack or as cocktail tidbits, and in cooked sauces. These will keep quite well in a canning jar standing on a dimly lit shelf in a cool place, but if you are at all uncertain as to the remaining moisture level, they keep just as well in the freezer.

Stuffed Dried Tomatoes

I have followed Patience Gray's directions for folding leathery dried tomatoes around bits of anchovies, capers, and fennel seeds like tiny sandwiches, tucking them tightly together in small jars, topping with a bay leaf, and then covering with olive oil before putting the lid on. I spend a good deal of my year finding the most beautiful half-pint jars in which to give these as gifts. They're received with wild acclaim — the perfect antipasto as well as that sublime mouthful you seek sometimes. If you make them, too, use one very small piece of anchovy, no bigger than half a dime, per tomato, one very large caper, two fennel seeds, and the very best olive oil you can find. Add to this a scattering of the best oil-cured olives that have been crushed by the side of a cleaver to pit them, perhaps a crumb of dried hot red pepper, as well as a curl of lemon or orange peel. Put the tops on the jars and refrigerate. Let them marinate in a cool place if you have a reliable one, or under refrigeration, for at least two weeks before tasting. You will find them mouthfuls of the most flagrantly exciting tastes. Give them as gifts, but be sure to keep a little jar for yourself. Gray advises, "Eat them with a glass of wine in winter."

Dried Tomato Harissa

This is a variation on the hot pepper harissa used in northern African cuisines. It is delightful on steamed vegetables, stirred into sauces, or thinned with broth to dress pasta. We prefer it uncooked, but others like it slathered thickly on a fish and roasted, or spread on good French bread and broiled.

Makes 1½ cups

2 ounces Vermont Oven-
   Dried Tomatoes —
   20 halves (p. 141)
2 large dried hot New
   Mexican chiles
1 chipotle
boiling water to cover
   (not more than
   1 cup)
2 garlic cloves, smashed,
   peeled, and cut into
   3 pieces
2 large salt-preserved
   anchovies (or 6 small
   oil-cured)

1 teaspoon cumin,
   ground or seeds
1 teaspoon coriander,
   ground or seeds
2 tablespoons red table
   wine
¼ cup virgin olive oil
1 heaping tablespoon
   olive puree (or 12 oil-
   cured black olives,
   smashed, pitted, and
   chopped)
salt to taste, if needed

In a small bowl soak tomatoes, chiles, and chipotle in the hot water for at least ½ hour or up to 6 hours. Drain and reserve both the chiles and tomatoes and the soaking liquid. Meanwhile, toast the cumin and coriander in a small pan over low heat until aromatic, shaking the pan frequently and watching carefully. Remove from the heat. Rinse and bone the anchovies if they are salt-preserved.

Into a blender, mortar, or bowl of a food processor, put the tomatoes, chiles, garlic, anchovies, spices, wine, ¼ cup of the soaking liquid, and the olives.

Process or pound until smooth. Add the olive oil and combine just until blended. Correct seasonings. Scrape the paste into a bowl or wide-mouthed pint canning jar, smooth the top, and carefully cover the entire surface with ¼ inch of olive oil to keep out air. Cover tightly and refrigerate. The harissa will keep a week or two if it remains covered with oil. Or freeze for later use.

Sweet Dried Tomato Figs

Another way of drying tomatoes is to stew them in sugar first, then dry in the sun or oven. This is an old technique that I found in Sarah Rorer's *How to Cook Vegetables*. That one treated 6 pounds of tomatoes, but I think 3 is enough to handle in today's kitchen. The tomato taste is concentrated but sweet, and children like them especially. This exotically old-fashioned treat adds panache to a dessert course of fruits, nuts, and cheeses, or a simple cup of tea. It is also used in a variation of Annie's Green Tomato Poundcake (p. 182).

3 pounds small, smooth, fresh plum tomatoes	**1½ pounds granulated sugar**

Scald and remove tomato skins, but don't core or mar in any way. Put tomatoes in a heavy-bottomed pan large enough to hold them in one layer. Strew with sugar and let them sit for 15 minutes or until the juices begin to run. Place over a moderate fire and stew very slowly "until the sugar appears to have penetrated the tomatoes," says Mrs. Rorer. When the smooth flesh on their undersides becomes a little ragged, apparently porous, take a slotted spoon and roll them over in their syrup and continue to stew until the whole tomato has that appearance. This step will take 20 minutes to ½ hour.

With the slotted spoon, carefully remove them from the syrup and place them on a wire rack over a baking sheet. Put them in the oven turned to the lowest heat. My electric oven barely registers 150 degrees. A gas oven with the pilot light on should be heat enough. Let them dry in that low oven for approximately 8 hours, turning them every hour or so, so that they dry evenly. When they are done, they will feel dry to the touch.

If you have the sun for it, most definitely dry them in the sun, but cover with cheesecloth or netting to keep the flies off. Mrs. Rorer adds, "Care must be taken not to let the rain or dew fall on them while drying."

Pack them in jars with layers of sugar in between.

Some Thoughts on Canning Tomatoes

And now we come to the real Tomato Imperative! Each morning we look out at the nasturtiums, almost hoping to see them turned to black mush, but there they are, only a shade less green, their yellow and orange and red blossoms transcending seasons. When I see this, my most favorite flower, surviving, what do I say? "Oh, no, more tomatoes!"

The scrawny, chill-scarred vines support ever-ripening fruits until the first hard frost turns them to mush. Chore, yes, and at the same time, blessing. No matter how they bury us at this season they remain the one staple that cannot be imported with any verisimilitude in winter, and so are to be, if not cherished, at least looked after. Each day we bring in the pink ones to ripen, until the zinc-topped cabinet is covered with fruits that have turned red and threaten to become wrinkled on their way to leaky at any minute — and they aren't the only fruits that are piled and stacked and contained, in all stages of ripeness, all over the garden and kitchen, demanding to be eaten, prepared, or preserved.

If you're like me, canning tomatoes brings to mind the eighteen-hour marathons put on by my mother and other female kin when I was a kid. On long, hot August days the big cookstove roared and the tomatoes, first in their skins and then in the jars, steamed up the big kitchen. Everything was steamy and red as though something passionate and dangerous was happening. The women gossiped and wiped things up with the tail ends of their aprons, swiped their foreheads with languid backs of wrists, tensed themselves to lift heavy copper boilers, and later on tightened the rings on crimson jars with checked dish towels. When the others went home, we were left with ranks of bright, jeweled jars.

Those jars and the communal aspect of the day made canning tomatoes a pleasurable duty; whereas making a clear and ruby and perfectly set currant jelly was a self-indulgence they would need to steal the time for.

My women kin skinned tomatoes and squashed the fat, juicy globes into the scalded jars, whole, then bathed them in boiling water for maybe twenty minutes. Sometimes my grandmother brought the tomatoes to a simmer, put them into the scalding hot jars, fished the lids from hot water, screwed on the rings, and set them aside to seal in their own heat. That simply won't do nowadays. Janet Greene has much to say on the ins and outs of canning tomatoes correctly in the fourth edition of *Putting Food By*. But in those innocently dangerous days, my mother canned green peppers and onions with tomatoes and, on winter evenings, would empty one of those jars into a saucepan, heat, and serve it as the evening's vegetable. We'd reach for the sugar bowl and stir quite a bit into the tomatoes, until they crunched when we ate them. James Beard's mother served her canned tomatoes topped with poached eggs, bits of butter, parsley, salt, and pepper, with buttered bread and good smoked ham.

Tomatoes can also be frozen. Our friend Carol Macleod pops them fresh from the garden into plastic bags and into the freezer. Or you can slice tomatoes in half and gently squeeze out the seeds before placing in plastic bags and freezing.

However it is that you've decided to preserve the contents of the garden in the plentitude of this season, we leave it to you to consult the experts, such as Janet Greene or the Ball Canning Jar folks, for explicit directions.

Jams and Condiments

Tomato Herb Jam

*I*F you grew up with them, you know immediately what to do with tomato jams — put them on your breakfast toast, of course. Tomato herb jams seem to adapt well to butterless toast in this new age of low fat, and they're particularly good on cornbread. They make an intriguing jelly roll, decorated with fresh leaves of the herb in question or served in the French way, as a dessert, with fresh cream cheese or plain pouring cream.

The technique of plunging a fragile, aromatic herb into simmering syrup just as it reaches the jelling point is timeless and very effectively preserves the taste and scent of the herb. It is nowhere more beautifully expressed than in Patience Gray's method for preserving basil in peach jam in her glorious book *Honey from a Weed.* It's a treasure of a preserve, one that's no less sensuous to make of tomatoes, with basil or thyme.

The jelling point is reached at 224 degrees on a candy thermometer, but we have surer luck when a spoonful of the jam, poured onto a cold plate, wrinkles rather than runs; or consult Janet Greene's *Putting Food By.* But make sure the jelling point is reached or the jam won't keep unless refrigerated.

Makes 6 half-pints

3 pounds ripe tomatoes	pinch of salt
1½ pounds sugar	1 large bunch of fresh
(2¾ cups)	basil, rinsed and
2 lemons	dried

149

Scald the tomatoes, slip them from their skins, slice them in half, and gently seed and juice. Cut them into a large, heavy-bottomed pan over low heat. Pour the sugar over the tomatoes, add the zest of one of the lemons, cut the lemons in half, squeeze the juice over the sugar, and sprinkle with salt. Stir over low heat until the sugar is melted. Raise the heat to medium high until the mixture is brought to a boil, then set to medium to keep it simmering, stirring intermittently until the jam reaches the jelling point. Take the pan from the heat. Divide the basil among scalded half- or quarter-pint jars and fill with the jam. Process in a boiling water bath for 15 minutes. Store in the refrigerator after opening.

Variation: Tomato Thyme Jam

Substitute ½ cup inexpensive red wine for the lemon juice and zest. Proceed as above, replacing the basil with 1 large bunch of fresh thyme.

Tomato Hot Tarragon Jam

On crackers with cream cheese, this saucy jam deliciously combines tomatoes' traditional companions — tarragon, the "little dragon," sometimes demands to breathe some fire, supplied here by the chipotles (smoke-dried jalapeños), to make an ideal barbecue sauce. Add more tarragon or another pepper, according to your desire. Dollop the jam on steamed carrots, beets, or butter-fried spring parsnips, add a bit of horseradish to it, and broil it over a wedge of Brie for a melty dip or brush it on partially roasted pork. It is used in Grilled Shrimp with Tomato Hot Tarragon Jam (p. 223) and Pan Chicken with Tomato Hot Tarragon Sauce (p. 221).

Makes 6 half-pints

2 cups inexpensive dry red wine	2 limes
3 pounds tomatoes	2 chipotles, crushed
1½ pounds sugar (about 2¾ cups)	pinch of salt
	1 large bunch of tarragon

Put the wine into a small saucepan, bring to a low boil, and reduce to ½ cup. Follow the method for Tomato Herb Jam (p. 149), incorporating the hot pepper, the zest of 1 lime, and the juice of both, along with the wine, in the cooking, which will take a bit longer due to the extra liquid. Plunge the tarragon in at the end and process as for Tomato Herb Jam.

Ketchup

Many countries have adopted some form of ketchup, both the word and the sauce, although only in comparatively recent times has it come to connote a sauce made of tomatoes. The original was probably made of fermented fish, come via travelers of some sort from the Cantonese district of China, where there was a condiment called kechap, to Malaysia and thence to Europe. At each stop it was made of such locally available ingredients as mushrooms and walnuts, and, notes the *American Heritage Dictionary,* in the eighteenth and nineteenth centuries ketchup (or catchup or catsup) was a generic term for sauces whose only common ingredient was vinegar. Our ketchup is a spicy mélange of flavors smoothed at the end with port wine, as suggested in old cookery books, and coming to resemble, finally, a sophisticated barbecue sauce. Roasting lets you cook this down until very thick with no danger of burning. As a gift, this could earn a lot of appreciation!

Makes 8 half-pints

6 quarts ripe, meaty tomatoes
2 sprigs of lovage or celery leaves
1 large, sharp white onion, cut in chunks
1 bay leaf
1 tablespoon lightly crushed mustard seeds
1 teaspoon mace
1 teaspoon minced gingerroot
1 tablespoon black pepper
1 small hot red pepper
2 teaspoons ground allspice
⅓ cup sugar
2 teaspoons salt (to taste)
1½ cups red wine vinegar
1 cup port wine, or to taste

Wash, core, and halve tomatoes, put into a large pot, and simmer them without stirring over medium-low heat for ½ hour or until they have given up their liquid. Heat oven to 375 degrees. Pour the liquid off the tomatoes and put them in a roasting pan with the lovage and onion, bay leaf, mustard seeds, mace, gingerroot, black pepper, hot pepper, allspice, sugar, salt, and vinegar and bake for 2 hours. Remove from the oven, lower heat to 325 degrees, and let the vegetables cool a bit. Ladle into the bowl of a food processor and chop in batches. Pour into a food mill and process to remove skins and seeds. Put the puree back into the roasting pan and bake, stirring occasionally, until very thick, perhaps 2 more hours. Remove from the oven, cool, add port wine to taste, put into jars, and process in a boiling water bath for 20 minutes.

Triple Red Chutney

Although this beautiful and complexly flavored chutney draws raves on its own, we paired it with the Roasted Green Tomato Salsa (p. 28) to complement the Hickory Grilled Pork Loin (p. 140) and were quite pleased with ourselves. You could can 2 half-pints of it and still have lots left over to eat by itself or to accompany a sandwich or grilled meats. Try some on top of cottage cheese for an intriguing little lunch.

Makes 1 quart or 4 half-pints

5 cups cored, coarsely
    chopped ripe
    tomatoes
4 cups seedless red
    grapes, rinsed
1 cup dried cranberries
    (or 2 cups fresh)
1 small dried hot
    pepper, minced
1-inch knob of
    gingerroot, peeled
    and smashed

1 large garlic clove,
    smashed and peeled
1 cup cider vinegar
¾ cup sugar
1 tablespoon salt
1 cinnamon stick
5 whole cloves

Combine all ingredients in a heavy-bottomed pot and stir well. Cover and bring to a boil over medium-high heat, then uncover and simmer until thickened, about 1½ hours. It stores well in a covered glass jar in the refrigerator for at least a month, or put in jars and process for 20 minutes in a boiling water bath.

Sweet and Sour Li'l Onions

Put this onion relish up now and eat it with the Thanksgiving turkey or with the end-of-summer pork roast, chutney fashion. The recipe is good for about 1 quart of condiment that will keep a week or two in the refrigerator, or process it in small jars in a boiling water bath for 20 minutes.

1½ pounds pearl onions
3 tablespoons olive oil
8 anchovy fillets, rinsed, patted dry, and finely chopped
5 cups chopped ripe tomatoes
4 fresh rosemary sprigs or 2 tablespoons rosemary needles

¼ cup dark brown sugar, packed
½ cup balsamic vinegar
½ cup raisins
several grinds of pepper

Trim root ends from onions and cut a crisscross ¼ inch deep into each onion. Bring a pot of water to a boil, add onions, and boil 2 minutes. Drain and slip off skins easily. Heat olive oil in a large skillet over medium heat, add anchovies and onions, and sauté for several minutes until onions are lightly browned. Add remaining ingredients, bring to a boil, lower heat, and simmer about 45 minutes, until onions are tender when pierced with a fork and sauce is syrupy.

Part 4

The Last Green Tomatoes

OVER THE LAST FEW YEARS we've learned to use as many green tomatoes at this time of the year as possible, for they are nothing if not seasonal. Although we hear that vines can be pulled hours before a hard frost and hung in the barn or the cellar, when we tried it we heard a steady "plop," "ploosh!" from their vicinity, the noise indicative of tomatoes dropping plushly onto the floor. Even if they had stayed on the vine and slowly reddened, the fact is that tomatoes picked green may ripen in color but not in taste, so we urge you to use as many as you can in the following dishes before the season is over. Extras can be stuffed into thick plastic bags and frozen, then released from their cold confinement in January to be used in soups and stews or other slowly cooked dishes to be found here. They will taste *almost* as tart and lemony as they do when fresh. Or prepare the dishes in early fall with fresh-from-the-garden produce and freeze large or small quantities for later use.

Green tomatoes can be found out of season if you know where to look. We've ordered pecks of them straight from Florida growers in January and February and been pleased with the result. However, this can be an expensive process that at the same time provides you with too many of the green things unless you are cooking for crowds, or unless you can share a case with several friends. Local produce distributors often supply restaurants with green tomatoes and sometimes will deal with individuals, to give them commonsense quantities.

But the best route is to enjoy them while they're in season.

Meals in a Bowl

South American Bean, Corn, and Squash Stew

ON a Technicolor autumn day, these vegetables could all be cooked fresh from the garden, then frozen, with the directions to wait for a chill day in February to thaw, combine with cooked pinto beans, and sprinkle with fresh cilantro, so you can enjoy treating yourself with the bright aroma and autumnal colors. Or you can make it and eat it now.

Serves 8 to 10

1 pound dried pinto beans

2 tablespoons vegetable oil

1 cup chopped onion

2 garlic cloves, smashed, peeled, and minced

1 cup chopped green pepper

1 teaspoon cumin seeds

1 tablespoon fresh oregano, or 1 teaspoon dried

½ teaspoon ground coriander

2 bay leaves

¼ teaspoon crushed dried hot red pepper

2 large green tomatoes, coarsely chopped (2 cups)

2 cups peeled, seeded, and chunked butternut squash

2 large ears of corn cut into 1-inch chunks

1 teaspoon salt

¼ teaspoon freshly ground pepper

½ cup minced fresh cilantro

Wash and pick over the beans, put them in a pot, cover them with water, and bring to a boil. Remove from heat, cover, and let sit for 1 hour. Or soak them at least 6 hours or overnight in cold water.

Heat the oil in a large casserole over medium-high heat, and sauté onion, garlic, pepper, cumin, oregano, coriander, bay leaves, and hot pepper for 5 minutes. Add the tomatoes, squash, corn, and beans with their liquid and bring to a boil. Lower heat and simmer until beans are tender, about 1 hour. Season to taste with salt and pepper, stir in cilantro, and serve.

Beans

Try different kinds of dried beans, alone or in combination — Baby Lima, Black-Eyed Peas, Yellow-Eyed Beans, Black Turtle, Navy, Great Northern, Soldier, Cranberry, Jacob's Cattle — all of whose flavors and textures we find to be very similar. But what different visual experiences they offer. To prepare: pick them over, rinse them under water, put them in a pan, cover them with cold water, and soak them for 6 hours or overnight. Or, after you've covered them with cold water, bring them to a boil for 2 minutes, remove from heat, and let them soak, covered, for 1 hour.

To discover the sturdy and pleasing flavor of the real bean, cook in plain water and season only with salt toward the end of cooking, when there is no danger of retarding their tenderness. Cook until they are tender but not falling apart, 45 minutes to 1½ hours. When they have cooled, dress them generously with good olive oil, salt and pepper, and chopped tomatoes as in Espey's Basic Salsa (p. 57). Once you have discovered their real identity, go boldly forward and cook them with a variety of flavorful fresh or dried hot and mild chiles to your own taste, just the way the ancient peoples would have made the first version of chili.

Corn, Green Tomato, and Ham Soup

Hearty, simple, warming — this soup just keeps getting better. Think of it when you have a good ham bone. It makes more than a gallon and can be frozen.

1 large, meaty ham bone	1 tablespoon dried
3 cups corn kernels	lovage leaves (or a
3 cups coarsely chopped	handful of fresh
green tomatoes	celery leaves)
2 cups peeled and	1 teaspoon dried thyme
coarsely chopped	1 tablespoon salt
carrots	¼ teaspoon black pepper
1½ cups coarsely	
chopped onion	

Place all the ingredients in a large pot with 12 cups of water. Bring to a boil, lower heat, and simmer for 2 hours. Remove the ham bone, cut off and dice any meat, skim off the surface fat from the soup, and put the meat in the soup. Correct the seasonings and serve.

Light Suppers

Succotash Salad with Okra

$\mathcal{W}$E were intrigued by the idea of green tomatoes in a succotash, but we weren't impressed with the hot dish. We wanted a little country ham taste that the bacon provides, and this is what Ruth came up with. It's delicious and easy to make from the late-season garden, and it makes enough to offer at a Labor Day potluck.

Serves 6 to 8

1½ cups baby lima beans
1½ cups corn kernels
1 cup thinly sliced okra
½ cup slivered red onion
½ cup celery in ¼-inch dice
⅓ cup red pepper in ¼-inch dice
1½ cups chopped green tomatoes
½ cup crumbled crisp-fried bacon

1 tablespoon pure Vermont maple syrup
2 teaspoons Dijon mustard
1 teaspoon salt
½ teaspoon freshly ground pepper
4 tablespoons cider vinegar
4 tablespoons light olive oil

Steam or parboil the beans, corn, and okra just until crisp/tender far enough in advance so that they have time to cool. Toss them together with the red onion, celery, pepper, tomatoes, and bacon in a serving bowl.

Whisk together the maple syrup, mustard, salt, pepper, vinegar, and olive oil and pour over the vegetables. Toss. Set aside at room temperature for an hour or so to let the flavors meld and vegetables macerate.

Green Tomatoes Stuffed with Corn and Cheese

These are yummy little gems with which to celebrate a late-summer supper in the kitchen.

Serves 4

4 large green tomatoes
1 teaspoon kosher salt
1⅓ cups corn kernels
6 tablespoons sour cream
¼ cup minced scallions
6 ounces shredded Monterey Jack cheese
1 teaspoon salt
¼ teaspoon ground pepper
2 long, green, mildly hot peppers, roasted, skinned, and chopped (or a 4-ounce can of chopped green chiles, drained)

Slice off the top of each tomato and scoop out the seeds and pulp with a melon baller or grapefruit knife. Sprinkle the insides of the tomatoes with the kosher salt and drain upside down for ½ hour. Preheat the oven to 350 degrees. Butter a 9-inch round baking dish. Mix corn, sour cream, scallions, cheese, salt, pepper, and green peppers or chiles together. Place the tomatoes in the baking dish and spoon the filling into them. Pour ½ inch of water around the tomatoes and bake 50 minutes or until tender when pierced with a fork. Don't overbake or the tomatoes will fall apart. Serve on a little bed of Peppy Slaw (p. 103), with warm, crusty bread.

Paella with Green Tomatoes and Bacon

If you have a paella pan (*paellera*), dig it out and use it, but otherwise use a large cast-iron skillet. Paella differs from risotto in that long-grain rice is usually called for, and the whole dish steams together rather than being stirred, which makes each grain of rice separate instead of creamy. Meld a pinch of saffron with a bit of warm broth and add it to the rice at the end if you like.

Serves 6 to 8

6 ounces bacon cut in ¼-inch strips	4 cups Rich Chicken Broth (p. 116)
1 cup chopped onion	1 teaspoon salt (decrease to ½ teaspoon if using canned broth)
1 cup green pepper cut in ½-inch dice	
2 garlic cloves, smashed, peeled, and minced	¼ teaspoon freshly ground pepper
1 jalapeño pepper, seeded and minced	1 tablespoon minced cilantro
2 cups long-grain rice	1 tablespoon minced Italian parsley
2 cups cored and coarsely chopped green tomatoes	

In a large, heavy-bottomed skillet render the bacon until it is brown and has released its fat. Discard all but 3 tablespoons of the fat. Stir in the onion, green pepper, garlic, and jalapeño and cook 7 to 8 minutes over medium heat until vegetables are wilted. Stir in the rice and cook for 1 minute longer. Add green tomatoes, broth, salt, and pepper, and bring to a boil. Cover, turn heat to very low, and cook about 20 minutes, until the rice has absorbed all the liquid. Fluff with a fork and stir in cilantro and parsley. Cover and let stand for 5 minutes before serving.

Sausage and Green Tomato Tart with Polenta

This can be a one-dish meal if you cook the sauce in an 8-inch or 9-inch cast-iron skillet or other ovenproof pan and top with the polenta, eliminating the need for a pie pan. You can crush the fennel seeds by leaning on a heavy cast-iron frypan placed over them. Make the polenta in a deep pot to protect yourself from hot splatters. Without the polenta this makes a delicate pasta sauce. Try it with ripe tomatoes, too, or a combination of the two. A small, velvety salad of Boston lettuce would be very nice with it.

Serves 4 as a main dish

1 pound sweet Italian sausage, casing removed	a few grinds of pepper
	⅔ cup masa harina or finely ground cornmeal
2 garlic cloves, minced	
½ teaspoon crushed fennel seeds	1 tablespoon butter
	½ cup plus 1 tablespoon freshly grated Parmesan
2 large green tomatoes (1 pound), chopped	
1 teaspoon salt	

Preheat oven to 425 degrees. Brown sausage in a 9-inch cast-iron skillet over medium-high heat, breaking up the meat with a fork as it browns. Add garlic, fennel, tomatoes, ½ teaspoon of the salt, and pepper. Lower heat, cover, and cook 15 to 20 minutes, until mixture forms a sauce. Remove from heat and set aside.

Bring 3 cups of cold water to a boil in a deep, heavy-bottomed pot over high heat, add remaining salt, and add the cornmeal in a slow steady stream, whisking it smooth. Turn the heat to medium and continue to cook and stir until the cornmeal is very thick, from 15 to 30 minutes. Remove it from the heat and stir in the butter and ½ cup of cheese. Spoon the polenta over sauce mixture in pan and sprinkle with the remaining tablespoon of cheese. Bake 20 minutes until brown.

Hearty Dinner Dishes

Lemongreen Braised Veal Shanks

*T*HIS and the following recipe reflect our intrigue with the Shaker method of rubbing a meat with salt, pepper, and sugar — sometimes with butter — then dredging it in a little flour before browning it, carefully, for the sugar increases the possibility of burning.

In this one, the flavor of butter enriches the veal, while the sugar and flour combine to give a nice caramel brown to it when cooked in olive oil. Building on that sweet with the flavorful sours of green tomatoes and lemon, you have a harmonious edifice. Serve the creamy sauce with fresh or dried noodles. Veal shanks are sometimes sold as *osso buco*.

Pasta

This is definitely worth making at home and, given the correct utensils, very easy, very simple. It's easy enough to mix up by hand, although I have used a food processor. The dough can even be rolled out by hand, but in that case get used to the idea of fat noodles, which are good and chewy. If you're going to make much of it, it's worthwhile to get a heavy-duty home pasta roller.

Makes about 12 ounces
of pasta

**2 cups hard wheat unbleached
    white flour (King Arthur
    is good)**
1 teaspoon fine salt
3 large eggs

Place the flour in a large mixing bowl or on a countertop. Sprinkle with the salt. Make a hollow in the middle of it and break the eggs into it. With a fork, begin to whip the eggs, incorporating the flour bit by bit until all is used.

166

Knead a few times with a pastry scraper until egg is incorporated and dough can be handled. Let rest for a few minutes, covered with a towel or plastic, if it is too brittle to knead. Then knead for about 10 minutes until it feels velvety and tough, like your grandmother's cheek, but also elastic, like your daughter's. Put it on the counter and throw a towel or a piece of plastic over it and let it rest for an hour.

Divide dough into four equal pieces. Take the first piece, sprinkle it with flour, and knead and roll it in your fingertips until smooth. If you are rolling it out by hand, you will need to let it rest a few minutes from time to time to allow it to lose a little of its elastic resistance before you continue rolling it. Fold the flour-dusted sheet back and forth like an accordion and slice to desired width. Unfold strips and hang over the handles of wooden spoons, which are secured by their bowls under something heavy at the edge of the counter. Let the strips dry at least 15 minutes. Continue with the other pieces. Or put each piece through each number of a pasta roller twice up to desired thickness. This takes a short time to cook in a large pot of boiling,

Serves 4

1 pound fresh or dried noodles
2 tablespoons olive oil
4 veal shanks (2 to 2½ pounds)
2 tablespoons butter, softened
1 teaspoon each salt and pepper
1 tablespoon sugar
⅓ cup flour
1 lemon
2 green tomatoes, cored and coarsely chopped
1 small fennel bulb, halved and sliced lengthwise

2 leeks, white and pale green parts only, halved through root end, cleaned, and sliced lengthwise
1 stalk of celery, thinly sliced
6 white mushrooms, thinly sliced
1 tablespoon fresh rosemary needles, or 1 teaspoon dried
1 cup dry white wine
salt and pepper to taste
½ cup heavy cream

If you are making homemade noodles, make the pasta dough now and let it rest while you make the following preparations.

In a large skillet, heat the olive oil over medium heat. Pat the veal shanks dry with paper towels. In a small bowl mash the butter with salt, pepper, and sugar, and with your fingers coat the shanks with the mixture. Sprinkle both sides of the shanks with the flour and pat it on to adhere, then tap excess off and place each shank in the hot oil. Brown slowly on all sides, shaking the pan and adjusting the heat so that they don't burn. This will take ½ hour to 45 minutes.

Meanwhile, zest the lemon in long strips and set aside. Shave off the bitter pith, slice the lemon thin, and discard the seeds along with the pith.

Over the thoroughly browned shanks, scatter in layers the lemon slices, tomatoes, fennel, leeks, celery, and mushrooms. Sprinkle rosemary and reserved lemon zest over, then the wine, turn heat to low, and cover the pan. Let simmer for ½ hour, or until the shanks and vegetables are quite tender and the vegetables and liquids have formed a sauce.

Remove the shanks from the pan and keep warm. Bring a pot of salted water to the boil for the pasta.

Fifteen minutes before serving, spoon off any surface fat, correct sauce seasonings, and stir in the heavy cream. Place shanks in the sauce, cover, and barely heat over low heat while you cook the pasta.

Green Tomato Pot Roast with Fall Vegetables

Surely there is historical precedent for including green tomatoes in pot roasts and someday, in some old cookbook, we'll find it. In the following dish the green tomatoes cook down into a wonderfully tart sauce. As in Fried Green Tomatoes (p. 25), salt and a judicious amount of fat combine well with "unripe" tomatoes.

Serves 6 to 8

4 pounds bottom round of beef

1 tablespoon each butter and vegetable oil

½ teaspoon each salt and pepper

1 teaspoon sugar

1 cup cider

3 garlic cloves, smashed, peeled, and chopped

1 teaspoon dried rosemary needles, crumbled, or 1 tablespoon fresh

2 large leeks, pale green and white parts, washed, quartered lengthwise, and cut into 1-inch lengths

1 small hot pepper, minced

2 large green tomatoes (1 pound), cored and cut into eighths

2 large carrots, pared and cut into ½-inch dice

1 large turnip, peeled and cut into ½-inch dice

3 to 4 medium-sized potatoes (1¼ to 1½ pounds), quartered

salt and pepper

1 large bunch of arugula

1 tablespoon flour

1 tablespoon butter

Pat the meat dry and rub into it the sugar, salt, and pepper. Put a large, heavy-bottomed pot over medium heat, and when it is hot drop the butter and oil into it. Brown the beef slowly on all sides, taking about half an hour. Add the cider to the pan, cover, and simmer over medium-low heat for 20 minutes. Meanwhile, prepare the vegetables, putting the carrots, turnip, and potatoes in a bowl with cold water to cover until needed. Turn the meat and add the garlic, rosemary, leeks, hot pepper, and green tomatoes to the pot. Cover and simmer for an hour or more, adding more cider if needed, until the meat begins to shred when the tines of a fork are twisted in it. Then add the carrots, turnip, and potatoes, season with salt and pepper, cover, and simmer until vegetables are tender, about 20 minutes. The meat should be very tender.

Wash the arugula and dry on paper towels, then chop coarsely and put into a large bowl. When the carrots, turnip and potatoes are tender, remove to the bowl and toss with the arugula. Keep warm. Remove the meat to a serving platter and keep warm. Spoon off any surface fat in the pan. Mash the butter with the flour and stir bits of it into the broth and cooked-down tomatoes still in the pan just to amalgamate the whole into a satiny sauce. If it's too thick, add a bit of water. Correct the seasonings.

To serve, slice meat thinly across the grain and arrange simply on a platter. Mound the vegetable mixture on either side and spoon the sauce over the meat. Serve immediately.

Chicken, Shrimp, and Buttermilk Pie

Just as last summer's Buttermilk Shrimp Soup (p. 32) is deliciously cooling, so this dish, for this season, is utterly warming and filling with the same creamy tang. Partially baking the biscuit before turning it onto the simmering pie keeps it from soaking up all the liquid. We always bone our own chicken, tossing the bones into a pan of cold water and bringing them to a simmer to make a quick, delicious broth. There are crockery bowls, glazed only on the inside, that seem to have been made specifically for deep-dish and pot pies, being 3½ to 4 inches deep. If you don't have one of these, you can use a 9-inch or 10-inch by 3-inch oval or round baking dish. On the off chance that you have leftovers to warm for a second-day serving, be sure to add more buttermilk, as we've noticed that its flavor is evanescent.

Serves 4 hearty eaters

2 whole chicken breasts (4 halves)	½ pound medium shrimp, peeled

For the biscuit:

2 cups all-purpose flour	2 tablespoons chopped fresh dillweed
2½ teaspoons baking powder	1 teaspoon pepper
½ teaspoon salt	⅓ cup unsalted butter, softened
½ teaspoon baking soda	¾ cup buttermilk

To assemble the pie:

2 tablespoons butter	2 tablespoons chopped fresh dillweed
2 large shallots, peeled and minced	2 tablespoons cornstarch
2 medium green tomatoes, cored and cut in thin crescents	¼ cup cooled chicken broth
½ teaspoon salt	½ cup hot chicken broth
½ teaspoon pepper	1 cup buttermilk

170

Remove the skin from the chicken breasts and discard. Separate the flesh from the bones, put the bones into a pot of cold water to cover, and bring to a simmer over medium heat but do not allow to boil. Simmer for 2 hours altogether (amounts needed in this recipe can be obtained after 45 minutes while the broth is still simmering). Let the rest cook, then cool, strain, and chill. Spoon off any congealed fat and discard, and use the broth as you will.

Remove fillets from the chicken breasts. Cut main part of breast into widths the size of the fillets and cut all the strips crosswise into large chunks. You should have 1½ pounds of chicken chunks. Put them in a bowl, cover with plastic wrap, and refrigerate until needed. Peel the shrimp and reserve.

Prepare the biscuit. Preheat the oven to 400 degrees. In a large mixing bowl, using a wooden spoon or a paddle, stir together flour, baking powder, salt, baking soda, dill, and pepper. Blend in the butter and then the buttermilk until the dough holds together stickily. Remove it from the bowl to a flour-sprinkled work surface and knead briefly. Roll or pat to a shape that will fit inside the top of your baking dish and place on a baking sheet. Bake for 10 minutes and remove from the oven, but leave the oven on.

Ladle ¼ cup of the hot broth into a small bowl and let cool.

In the meantime, melt the 2 tablespoons of butter in a large sauté pan over medium-low heat. Add the shallots and allow to wilt. Add the tomatoes, salt, pepper, and 1 tablespoon of the dill. Stir, cover, and cook for 5 minutes. Stir in the chicken chunks. Cover and cook for 10 more minutes, stirring occasionally.

Mix the cornstarch in the ¼ cup of cooled broth and stir it into the pan with the chicken. Add the ½ cup of hot chicken broth and stir in the buttermilk and the shrimp. Heat and stir over low heat until thickened, correct seasonings, then pour into the baking dish.

Sprinkle with the remaining dill, cover with the partially baked buttermilk biscuit, and slip it into the oven for 10 to 15 minutes or until liquids are bubbling and the biscuit is browned. Remove from the oven, allow to set for 10 minutes, then serve.

Preserves and Condiments

Green Tomato Walnut Conserve

CONSERVES and mincemeats of green tomatoes are commonly known to households stemming from a northern European tradition, and can be a particular treat to people who recall the memorable tastes from childhood.

Make some whole-wheat pancakes and dollop them with this conserve. Or put a spoonful in the middle of a pretty dish and drizzle it with Crème Fraîche (p. 56), yogurt, or just very thick sweet cream to end a meal nicely.

Makes 10 cups

5 cups green tomatoes
  (2 pounds), cored
  and coarsely chopped
1½ pounds seedless
  green grapes, rinsed
5 cups Granny Smith
  apples, cored and
  diced, but not peeled

1½ cups sugar
1⅓ cups apple cider
1½ cups walnut pieces,
  toasted

Place tomatoes, grapes, apples, sugar, and apple cider in a heavy-bottomed pot and bring slowly to a boil over medium heat, stirring occasionally with a wooden spoon. Lower the heat slightly, stir occasionally, and keep the mixture at a fast simmer for 1¼ hours, until it is very thick. Stir the walnuts in and cool.

It will keep in the refrigerator in a covered glass container for at least a month; or you can can it in half-pint jars in a boiling water bath for 20 minutes, if you want to keep it longer or give it as a holiday gift.

Quigley's English Marmalade

A tangy, fruity, English-style marmalade that needs to mellow in the jar for at least a month before using or giving as an excellent gift.

Makes 4 pints

3 pounds green tomatoes, cored and quartered (6 cups)	2 oranges
	½ cup lemon juice
	1 teaspoon pectin (we like Pomona's Universal Pectin)
3 cups sugar	
2 limes	
2 lemons	

Puree the tomatoes with the sugar in the bowl of a food processor and put the mixture into a heavy-bottomed pot. Remove the zest from the limes, lemons, and oranges with a zester or with a swivel-bladed peeler. If using the latter, finely shred the zest. Remove and discard all the white pith from the fruit and coarsely chop the fruit. Add it, along with the zest, to the tomatoes. Cook over medium heat, stirring occasionally, for 45 minutes or until very thick. Stir the pectin with the lemon juice until smooth, add to the marmalade, and cook 1 minute longer. Pour into sterilized pint jars and process in a boiling water bath for 10 minutes.

Green Tomato Mincemeat

My grandmother made such wonderful mincemeat out of beef or venison neck meat that I had always prided myself on making only that kind of mincemeat before we wrote this book. Then I realized I would have to give this a try, and guess what? It's delicious—yummy as an accompaniment to meat, and it has a great affinity for cream cheese when spread on thin slices of brown bread. Most wonderfully of all, it is used in the filling of the Italian Green Tomato Mincemeat Tart (p. 179). The suet gives it a special flavor, but if you wish to omit it you can substitute butter. It keeps practically forever in the refrigerator, but you should can it in pint jars in a boiling water bath for 20 minutes to be safe.

Makes about 4 cups; can be doubled

2 ounces beef suet, chopped

3 green tomatoes (1 pound), cored and chopped

1 Granny Smith apple, chopped

zest and juice of 1 lemon

zest and juice of 1 lime

¼ cup cider vinegar, cider, or hard cider

1 quarter-sized round of fresh gingerroot, smashed and chopped

½ teaspoon freshly grated nutmeg

½ onion, sliced in 1-inch shards

1¼ cups brown sugar

1 teaspoon cinnamon

1 teaspoon ground coriander

½ teaspoon salt

¼ cup golden raisins

¼ cup dry sherry

4 tablespoons pine nuts, toasted

In a large, heavy-bottomed pan, render the suet over medium heat until crackling. Stir in green tomatoes, apple, zests and juices, vinegar, gingerroot, nutmeg, onion, brown sugar, cinnamon, coriander, and salt. Cook over low heat with the cover cocked, stirring often, for about ½ hour.

Meanwhile, put raisins to macerate in the sherry.

When the mincemeat is thick and syrupy, correct seasonings and stir in the raisins, sherry, and pine nuts.

Leatha's French Pickle

We had this first when our friend Sharon Pressly served a perfectly done loin of pork with a selection of condiments of which this was our favorite. When we make it, everyone yells for hot dogs, as it is also the perfect hot-dog relish.

This is named after Sharon's mother's next-door neighbor in Ohio, and is also called green sauce, although ours turns out more brown than green because of the spices. In order to supply everyone who loves it, Sharon's mother, Pat Lipstreu, makes an extra-large batch every year, which takes 4 days. We make only 5 half-pints, which does not take long at all. You do not want to use a food processor to grind the ingredients, but an old-style, clamp-on, meat grinder.

Makes 5 half-pints

2 quarts green tomatoes (2½ pounds), cored and quartered	¾ pound dark brown sugar
1 large onion, quartered	¼ cup mustard seeds
1 large green pepper, seeded and quartered	¾ teaspoon ground cloves
¼ cup kosher salt	¾ teaspoon cinnamon
3 cups cider vinegar	¾ teaspoon ground black pepper

Grind the tomatoes with the onion and pepper. In a glass, plastic, or crockery bowl, toss the mixture with the salt, cover, and set aside overnight. Next morning, pour into a cloth-lined colander and drain well. Put it into a pot and add 1 cup of the vinegar and 2 cups of water, bring to a boil over medium heat, and cook 15 minutes. Pour it back into the cloth-lined colander and drain well. Return it to the pot, add the remaining 2 cups of vinegar, sugar, mustard seeds, cloves, cinnamon, and black pepper, and bring it back to a boil over medium heat. Cook 20 minutes, stirring occasionally. Spoon into sterilized half-pint jars and process in a boiling water bath for 10 to 15 minutes. Age at least 2 weeks before serving.

Desserts

Green Tomato Upside-Down Cake

*T*HIS is a charming dish that came about when Ruth was experimenting with a green tomato tarte Tatin. When the tomatoes proved too liquid for a pastry crust, she decided to try a "biscuit," which turned out to be a shortcake. This is a handsome Old World dessert in appearance and on the tongue.

Ruth distractedly grated lemon rind directly over the brown sugar in the baking pan instead of into the cake ingredients, and we decided to keep it that way.

Serves 8 to 10

2 tablespoons unsalted
   butter, softened
¾ cup dark brown sugar,
   packed
1 lemon
3 cups (1½ pounds)
   small green tomatoes
   cut in thin wedges
2¼ cups all-purpose
   flour

¼ cup sugar
1¼ teaspoons baking
   powder
½ teaspoon baking soda
¼ teaspoon salt
6 tablespoons unsalted
   butter
1½ cups buttermilk

Heat oven to 375 degrees. Spread the softened butter on the bottom and sides of a 10-inch by 2-inch round cake pan. Sprinkle brown sugar evenly over the bottom. Grate the rind of the lemon evenly over the sugar. Overlap the wedges of tomato in concentric circles over all.

Stir the flour, sugar, baking powder, baking soda, and salt together, and cut in the butter with a pastry cutter or with your fingers until the mixture resembles oatmeal. Stir in the buttermilk. Pour the batter into the pan over the tomato topping and bake until golden brown and a pick inserted in the center comes out dry, about 45 minutes.

Let cool about 20 minutes and invert onto a serving platter. Serve warm with a scoop of Crème Fraîche (p. 56).

Italian Green Tomato Mincemeat Tart

This handsome rustic pie would not be out of place on a holiday table. When it is taken from the pan and placed on a pretty plate, the top fits over the bottom like the lid of a pot. It is no more beautiful than it is delicious. A slender slice succinctly complements slivers of roast meats, as well as finishes a meal. There are three steps involved, but the Italian pastry and mincemeat can be made ahead of time, preparatory to assembling the tart. To remove the tart from the pan bottom easily, use a flat piece of metal such as another tart-pan bottom or a sharp-edged baking sheet without a rim to slip between bottom crust and pan.

Serves 8 to 10

Italian sweet pastry dough:

2⅓ cups flour
⅓ cup sugar
½ teaspoon salt
grated zest of 1 lemon
¾ cup cold unsalted
    butter, cut into bits

1 large egg plus 1 egg
    yolk
1 teaspoon vanilla

Cream cheese layer:

4 ounces cream cheese
2 tablespoons honey
1 egg, beaten
1 tablespoon whole milk
grated zest of ½ lemon

½ teaspoon vanilla
¼ teaspoon freshly grated
    nutmeg
2 cups Green Tomato
    Mincemeat (p. 174)

In a large bowl, whisk together the flour, sugar, salt, and zest. Cut the butter in with a knife or pastry cutter, then rub the mixture quickly between your palms until it is the texture of cornmeal. In a small bowl, whisk together the egg, yolk, and vanilla. Add the egg mixture to the flour mixture and toss until incorporated. If you are using a food processor, pulse flour, sugar, salt, and lemon zest just until combined, then add the cold butter, the egg and yolk, and the vanilla, then pulse several times just until combined and only beginning to come together in a ball.

Turn onto a work surface, knead lightly with the heel of your hand to distribute the egg, form the dough into 2 disks, one slightly larger than the other, wrap in plastic wrap, and refrigerate for at least 1 hour.

Preheat the oven to 350 degrees. Roll out the larger portion of pastry and with it line a 10-inch, fluted, removable-bottom tart pan. Press excess pastry back into the fluted sides, pinching the two layers together and forming a ¼-inch margin above the edge to allow for shrinkage.

Blend the cream cheese with the honey until soft, add 2 tablespoons of the beaten egg, the milk, zest, vanilla, and nutmeg, and mix but do not beat. Pour into the pastry-lined pan and spread evenly. Bake the pie for about 20 minutes or until just set.

Meanwhile, roll out the top crust and prick it several times, decoratively, with a fork.

Remove the pan from the oven and let cool for 5 minutes. Carefully spread the Green Tomato Mincemeat over the cream cheese layer in the pan. Drape the top pastry over a rolling pin and carefully lower over the pan. Arrange it evenly and then run the rolling pin across the top of the pan to seal the edges and trim top crust exactly evenly. Brush with the remaining egg. Bake until the top is delicately golden, about 20 minutes.

Let cool and remove from pan to serving platter.

Serve in wedges, warm, with a spoonful of Crème Fraîche (p. 56).

Green Tomato and Fig Bundt Cake

Knowing how much I like figs, Ruth brought this cake to dinner one night. It's high and mighty, a handsome cake, richly brown, crunchy with figs, and moistly tart with green tomatoes.

Serves 16 generously

3 cups cake flour	2 cups dark brown sugar
2 teaspoons baking powder	1 cup vegetable oil
¾ teaspoon baking soda	3 eggs
¼ teaspoon salt	2 cups green tomato puree
½ teaspoon cinnamon	1½ cups chopped walnuts
½ teaspoon fresh ground nutmeg	confectioners' sugar
½ teaspoon allspice	
1 8-ounce package dried Calimyrna figs, diced (1½ cups)	

Preheat the oven to 350 degrees. Grease and flour a 12-cup bundt pan. Sift together the flour, baking powder, baking soda, salt, cinnamon, nutmeg, and allspice and set aside. Put the diced figs into a bowl and toss with 2 tablespoons of the flour mixture. Reserve. In the large bowl of an electric mixer cream together sugar and oil, beat in the eggs and green tomato puree, then stir in the flour mixture just until moistened. Stir in the chopped walnuts and the figs, pour into the bundt pan, and bake for 1¼ hours, or until a toothpick inserted in the center of the cake tests dry. Let cool in the pan before inverting on a serving platter. Sprinkle with confectioners' sugar before serving.

Annie's Green Tomato Poundcake

The idea for this came from our friend Annie Roberts, who baked green tomatoes and walnuts into quick bread. Our rich Breton poundcake, buttery and crisp around the edges, is no less friendly. The tomatoes give it a tang and a moistness that threatens—if it is not baked long enough—to make it stay too moistly caky in the lower third of the pan, but it is nonetheless delicious for that trait. Be sure to toss the tomatoes with some of the flour before adding. And make an extra cake to freeze or give as a gift. It has the richness of a fruitcake, so slice it thin.

Serves 8 to 10

⅓ cup sultanas (golden raisins)

¼ cup dark rum

1 large green tomato (8 ounces), cored, halved, seeded, and diced

½ teaspoon salt

1 teaspoon butter for pan

6 large egg yolks

2¼ cups all-purpose flour

1 cup sugar

1 cup unsalted butter at room temperature

2 tablespoons orange zest

½ cup walnut halves, toasted

Pour the rum over the raisins in a small bowl and set aside for at least 15 minutes. Prepare the tomato, put the dice into a large sieve, sprinkle with ¼ teaspoon salt, toss gently, and let drain.

Preheat the oven to 325 degrees and butter a 4-inch by 8-inch loaf pan.

In a small bowl, beat the egg yolks until thick and lemon-colored. Place 2 cups of the flour and remaining salt in a large bowl, make a well, put the sugar and butter in the middle, and with your fingers or the paddle attachment of your mixer work those ingredients well into the flour. Add the egg yolks (reserving a bit for glaze), raisins, rum, and orange zest and work in gently until the dough is smooth, if stiff. Toss the drained tomato with the remaining ¼ cup flour and gently work it, along with the walnuts, into the dough. Pat the dough into the cake pan and press out to the edges of the pan. Brush the top with the reserved egg yolk. You can make a simple design in the top of the cake with a fork or the back of a knife if you like. Bake for 1½ hours or until a knife inserted in the middle comes out clean. Allow to cool completely before removing from the pan.

Variation: For Tomato Fig Poundcake, substitute 4 to 6 Sweet Dried Tomato Figs (p. 146), cut in small dice, and ½ cup toasted pine nuts for the green tomatoes and walnuts.

Part 5

Summer into Winter

IT IS ONLY WHEN YOU stop to think seriously about it that you realize that tomatoes are omnipresent in dishes of distinction year-round. It's time now to use them in warming dishes that become heartier as the days and months pass. In these dishes we use late-season tomatoes, meaty plum tomatoes that come from gardens farther and farther away as the cold season progresses south, and finally we begin to break into the treasured ranks of our own canned tomatoes, or those from Dei Fratelli, Furmanos, or Del Monte.

Sometimes in February we'll happen upon a good-looking tomato that came from some far-flung corner of the universe and that may taste almost as good as it looks. In April or May South Carolina tomatoes begin their wonderfully long season, or seasons, and perhaps we'll get a few of them to taste. New Jersey, Michigan, and finally Vermont won't have garden-fresh tomatoes again until at least July.

The winter we spent testing these late-season dishes we used mostly meaty plum tomatoes, ordered directly from the most reputable growers and distributors we could find, and we used a lot of our own and commercially canned ones.

Some Notes on Canned Tomatoes

We all use them, and if you don't grow your own to put up for winter use, then buy the sweetest-tasting brand you can find in your region, for besides the nationally and internationally known brands there are many regional packers, as well as those packed under supermarkets' private labels.

We did our own tasting of fifteen different brands of canned tomatoes, including whole, crushed, and plum (Italian style), packed in puree and packed in juice, that were available in the three supermarkets in our immediate area. No imports were available, although we understand that Fara San Martino San Marzano Plum Tomatoes, packed in Italy, are choice when they can be

Appetizers

Wild Mushroom Toasts

found at a cost less than Midas's gold.

The best we found was Dei Fratelli brand, with no salt added, which tasted like home-canned tomatoes. Redpack and Furmanos were also good. Many of the others were too salty or unpleasantly sour. All except Dei Fratelli had salt, calcium chloride or calcium sulfide, and citric acid in them. Our local health food store carries the organic Muir Glen. A 28-ounce can of whole or crushed tomatoes yields 3⅓ cups.

WE invited friends to an all-tomato dinner, each to invent or test a recipe — tomatoes in every course — when I stumbled across a patch of the delectable wild shaggymane mushroom. I would build an edifice of them on little garlic toasts, capturing their fleeting delicacy between strains of cream and garlic, and combine them with the tangy, tiny, sweet orange tomatoes I had been finding at the farmers' market all summer. I sautéed the mushrooms with the aromatics, added a bit of cream, massed this on toasts, touched them with Parmesan, and ran them under the broiler. They were gobbled up by guests, and only as they reached for seconds did the chorus arise: "So, where are the tomatoes?" I'd forgotten them!

Fill a small earthen crock with small golden tomatoes or with a variety of tiny tomato shapes, colors, and flavors and put it out handy for people to snack from.

Makes 12 appetizers

1 to 2 tablespoons olive oil

1 large (double) shallot, peeled and minced

2 or 3 garlic cloves, smashed, peeled, and minced

½ pound wild mushrooms — shaggymanes, oysters, chanterelles, hen of the woods, or sulfur shelf would be optimum

⅛ cup dry sherry

approximately ⅔ cup light cream

coarse salt and freshly ground pepper to taste

¼ teaspoon freshly grated nutmeg

12 thin slices French bread

12 small, golden sweet tomatoes, quartered lengthwise in crescents

¼ cup freshly grated Parmesan

In a medium-sized sauté pan over a medium flame, heat the oil. Add shallot and garlic just to brown. Clean the mushrooms, inspecting every crevice, without resorting to running water if possible. Shred them and toss with the olive oil, shallot, and garlic. They will absorb the oil, and you can add a little more if you need to. They will give off their liquid and then it will disappear and the mushrooms will begin to brown just a bit. Immediately add the sherry, and when that is absorbed pour in the cream and stir the mixture over very low heat just until thickened. Add salt and pepper to taste and a scant grinding of nutmeg just to scent the mixture. Take from the heat and reserve.

Arrange the bread slices on a cookie sheet and run them under the broiler until they are lightly golden on one side. Take from the oven, turn the slices, arrange 4 tomato crescents on each slice, divide the mushroom mixture evenly over the tomatoes, sprinkle with Parmesan, give a final grind of pepper over the tops, and run under the broiler just until heated and cheese begins to melt. Arrange the toasts on a pretty serving dish and pass among your guests — with a little crock of extra tomatoes if you wish.

The Gathering and Care of Mushrooms

We collect wild mushrooms very, very carefully, concentrating only on those we surely recognize. These include the spring morels (which I've gathered since childhood), chanterelles in midsummer, shaggymanes in early fall, oysters all through, then the hen of the woods and sulfur shelf from late summer to late fall. These are all utterly delicious and worth learning about if you have a chance. All but the rapidly decaying shaggymanes are available, from time to time at least, in supermarkets or specialty stores. If you don't trust yourself — and you shouldn't — you might ask your favorite restaurant owner or chef to give you the name of a reputable gatherer in your locale. Seeing them in their own habitat, with someone who knows them, is the only safe way to recognize them.

Sometimes only one or two wild mushrooms are enough to flavor commercial button mushrooms when sautéed together.

To clean mushrooms:

Trim earthy ends and brush off any debris with a soft brush or the slanted blade of a paring knife. If you must wash them, toss carefully from hand to hand under cold running water, then blot dry with towels.

Strudel of Sundried Tomatoes and Cabbage

The air is brisk and the leaves are at the height of their color when suddenly you are seized with a craving for something cabbagy, and that is a good time to start with our Strudel of Sundried Tomatoes and Cabbage. Here, the earthy cabbage finds itself in the company of elegant phyllo pastry.

Makes 16 appetizer servings

4 tablespoons vegetable oil	1 teaspoon salt
2 cups sliced onion	⅛ teaspoon freshly ground pepper
2 green peppers, sliced in strips (2 cups)	12 sundried tomatoes, soaked in 1 cup hot water for ½ hour
6 cups coarsely chopped cabbage	1 tablespoon chopped fresh dill
1 teaspoon crushed caraway seeds	1 tablespoon flour
1 teaspoon sweet paprika	1 tablespoon butter
¼ teaspoon hot paprika	12 sheets phyllo pastry

Heat 2 tablespoons oil in a large skillet over medium heat and add onion, peppers, cabbage, caraway seeds, paprikas, salt, and pepper to the pan. Cook, stirring, for 2 minutes. Cover and cook until vegetables are wilted and browned, about 20 minutes. Drain the tomatoes, reserving the liquid, and chop fine. Uncover the pan and stir in the tomatoes and dill. Sprinkle the flour over the vegetables and stir for 1 minute, then stir in the reserved soaking liquid. Cook 2 to 3 minutes, until mixture is thickened. Correct seasonings and let cool.

Preheat oven to 350 degrees and prepare the phyllo. Melt the butter with the remaining 2 tablespoons oil. Place 3 sheets of phyllo on waxed paper while keeping the rest covered with a damp towel or plastic. Brush the top sheet with the butter/oil mixture and spread ¼ of the cabbage mixture along the long side facing you, leaving a 1-inch margin along the side facing you and

To dry mushrooms:

Drying intensifies their flavors and renders them keepable. I have good luck placing them on unglazed tiles, which absorb their moisture. When dry, place in a plastic bag and keep them in the freezer absolutely indefinitely.

To refresh dried mushrooms:

Pour hot water over to cover and let soak for 20 minutes to ½ hour. Strain any sand out of the flavorful soaking liquid by pouring it through several layers of cheesecloth, a paper towel, or a coffee filter before using.

See Mail-Order Sources (p. 243) for places that supply mushrooms.

the right and left sides, with a much larger margin at the top. Fold ends in over cabbage, then fold long edge over cabbage and roll it over and over to make a log. Place seam side down on a buttered baking sheet and brush with the butter/oil mixture. Repeat with remaining phyllo and filling to make four logs. With a sharp knife slash each log diagonally into quarters, but do not cut all the way through. Place in the oven and bake until golden brown, 35 to 40 minutes. Remove, cool 10 minutes, then cut through the slashes to make serving portions.

Fall Soups

Beef Broth

Once or twice a year we take veal knuckles and marrow bones and any other beef bones we've collected — 10 to 15 pounds of them — out of the freezer, buy a nice chuck roast, and start roasting them with root vegetables and aromatics. Next day they all go into the enormous broth pot with cold water, to come to a simmer, never to boil, to make a beef broth you can freeze and that will last the rest of the year.

It can be cooked down until very thick if you lack freezer space, then reconstituted when used.

Cabbage and Potato Soup

*T*HE combination of cabbage and potatoes may have originated in Ireland; add tomatoes and you've got something from heaven. When this craving hits, I usually make a simple cabbage soup out of whatever I have on hand, layering ingredients over low heat in a technique that lets each flavor slowly release itself to the others. It's loved by small children and authentic old curmudgeons alike.

Serves 4 to 6

2 tablespoons olive oil
2 large garlic cloves, smashed, peeled, and chopped
1 large onion, peeled and chopped
½ pound very lean ground pork
1 small hot pepper (or to taste), chopped, or crumbled if dried
1½ cups chopped late-season vegetables (carrot, eggplant, fennel, sweet pepper, or any other vegetable that pleases you)
2 large potatoes, cut in ½-inch dice or smaller
2 large ripe tomatoes, seeded and chopped (2 cups)
2 cups shredded cabbage
1 teaspoon salt
½ teaspoon pepper
4 cups Beef Broth, preferably homemade
2 tablespoons flavored vinegar — thyme or fennel
Crème Fraîche (p. 56), sour cream, or yogurt

191

Heat the olive oil over medium heat in a large sauté pan, strew in the garlic and onion, and stir for a moment until they are slightly limp. Crumble the ground meat into the pan and mix with the onion and garlic. Add the hot pepper to taste and stir until the meat is just pink on the way to being browned. Layer in the mixed vegetables and over them the potatoes, then the tomatoes, then the cabbage, and sprinkle with the salt and pepper. Cover and simmer until the cabbage is limp and the potatoes are tender, 20 minutes, then stir in the Beef Broth. Heat, season to taste, and add the vinegar. Serve in bowls topped with spoonfuls of Crème Fraîche or sour cream or even yogurt, with crusty bread on the side.

Spiced Whole Pea Soup

When you can find whole dried peas, they are intriguing to use. I prefer their texture to split, as the center holds together nicely, but in my experience finding them is usually a fluke. I think mine came from a Mennonite store in Virginia called Yoder's Country Market. I like a country ham end because the meat is glazed brown by the smoking, hard and lean; this type also comes from Virginia. When I visit friends there, I stock up with ham hocks and other seasoning products, dry-smoked and shrink-wrapped. You could serve this soup with a spoonful of Crème Fraîche (p. 56) on top if you were so inclined or a little yogurt, or stir buttermilk into it or drop some croutons or a few shavings of Parmesan on top, or even simmer small dumplings in it.

FALL SOUPS

Serves 6 to 8

3 tablespoons olive oil
1 cup sliced onion
3 garlic cloves, smashed,
   peeled, and chopped
1 or 2 chipotles,
   according to taste
ham end with bone,
   about 1 to
   1½ pounds, trimmed
   of fat
1 cup dry red table wine
3 large tomatoes
   (1½ pounds), chunked

2 teaspoons roasted and
   cracked cumin seeds
2 teaspoons ground
   coriander
1 pound dried peas,
   whole or split
1 teaspoon salt
freshly ground pepper
1 large russet-type
   potato, cut in very
   small dice

In a large saucepan or small soup pot heat the oil over medium heat and drop in the onion and garlic. Crush the chipotles with the side of a cleaver or chop and add to the pan. Stir for a few minutes until the onion is limp, then add the ham and cook it, turning it so that all sides come in contact with the vegetables and oil, for about 20 minutes. Then add the wine, the tomatoes, breaking them up with the edge of a wooden spoon if necessary, the cumin and coriander, and 6 cups of cold water. Cover and simmer for 30 minutes.

Pick over the peas, rinse in cold water, and add to the pot. Simmer until they are just tender — ½ to 1 hour — taste, and add salt and a few grinds of pepper as needed or to taste. Remove the meat from the bone, shred it, and return it to the soup with the diced potato. Simmer until potato is tender, about 20 minutes. Again, taste for seasonings and correct.

Double Mushroom and Tomato Soup

Here is a simple soup to serve with strong cheese and peasant bread for a hearty meal.

Serves 4 to 6

½ ounce dried
    mushrooms (p. 189)
1 tablespoon butter
1 tablespoon vegetable
    oil
1 cup chopped onion
3 cups (8 ounces) sliced
    white button
    mushrooms

3 large ripe tomatoes
    (3⅓ cups), peeled,
    seeded, and
    chopped — or 1
    28-ounce can whole
    peeled tomatoes in
    their own juices
1½ teaspoons salt
¼ teaspoon freshly
    ground pepper
1 tablespoon minced
    parsley

Soak the dried mushrooms in 4 cups of hot water for ½ hour. Melt the butter with the oil in a large soup pot and sauté the onion over medium heat until well browned. Add the fresh sliced mushrooms and cook 5 minutes, stirring. Remove the dried mushrooms from their soaking liquid with a slotted spoon, chop fine, and stir into the onion mixture. Strain the soaking liquid through a colander lined with a paper towel and add it to the pot along with the tomatoes and their juices, salt, and pepper. Simmer for 20 minutes. Sprinkle with parsley and serve.

Southwestern Pumpkin Tomato Soup

Ruth serves this often to family and friends, particularly on chilly fall days, when it is tremendously satisfying.

Serves 4 to 6

2 tablespoons vegetable oil
½ cup chopped onion
1 teaspoon minced garlic
1 crushed chipotle or ¼ teaspoon crushed red pepper or to taste
½ teaspoon ground cumin
¼ teaspoon ground coriander
1 bay leaf
3 cups peeled, cubed pumpkin or butternut squash

1½ cups chopped fresh tomatoes
1 cup Rich Chicken Broth (p. 116)
1 teaspoon salt
¼ teaspoon freshly ground pepper
6 tablespoons sour cream
6 tablespoons minced cilantro
6 tablespoons toasted pumpkin seeds (see p. 40)

Heat oil in a heavy-bottomed pot and sauté onion, garlic, chipotle, cumin, coriander, and bay leaf until the onion wilts, about 7 minutes, stirring occasionally. Add the pumpkin, tomatoes, Chicken Broth, salt, and pepper, and bring to a boil. Lower heat and simmer about 25 to 30 minutes, until pumpkin is tender. Remove bay leaf and puree the soup in a blender or pass through a food mill. Correct seasonings and serve in bowls with a spoonful of sour cream and sprinklings of cilantro and toasted pumpkin seeds.

Tricolori Soup

Make this jeweled soup with the first of the winter squash and the last of the fresh tomatoes and enjoy the harmony of all the individual taste notes, colors, and textures.

Makes 6 cups

1 tablespoon olive oil
2 teaspoons minced
   garlic
2 cups peeled butternut
   squash cut into
   ½-inch chunks
1 tablespoon chopped
   fresh sage or 1
   teaspoon dried
4 cups Rich Chicken
   Broth (p. 116)
1½ teaspoons salt

¼ teaspoon freshly
   ground pepper
1 cup fresh ripe
   tomatoes, peeled,
   seeded, and chopped
1 15-ounce can
   cannellini beans,
   drained and rinsed
1 tablespoon chopped
   fresh parsley
½ cup freshly grated
   Parmesan cheese

Heat oil in a large pot and sauté garlic for 1 minute over medium heat. Add squash and sage and stir for 1 minute. Add Chicken Broth, salt, and pepper. Bring to a boil, lower heat, and simmer 15 minutes until squash is tender. Stir in tomatoes, beans, and parsley and simmer 5 minutes longer. Serve topped with cheese.

Golden Harvest Soup

Chestnuts and golden tomatoes — sweetly savory and, yes indeed—golden! Remember to start soaking the chestnuts, which are available in health food and Chinese produce stores, the night before.

Serves 8 to 10

4 ounces dried chestnuts	1 teaspoon salt
6 leeks, 1 inch in diameter	5 large yellow tomatoes, chopped (5 cups)
4 tablespoons butter	2 cups chicken or turkey broth
3 cups (1½ pounds) peeled, seeded, and cubed butternut squash	1 cup heavy cream
	⅛ teaspoon freshly ground pepper

The night before serving, pour 2 cups of boiling water over the chestnuts and let them soak overnight. Next day, drain the chestnuts, reserve the liquid, pick off any remaining brown skin, and coarsely chop them.

Wash the leeks very well to remove any sand and chop the white and pale green parts. Melt the butter in a large, heavy-bottomed Dutch oven, add the chestnuts, leeks, squash, and salt, and cook, covered, for 35 to 40 minutes until tender. Add the tomatoes, broth, soaking liquid, and pepper and bring to a boil uncovered. Lower the heat and simmer for 30 minutes for flavors to blend. Pass the soup through a food mill, stir in the heavy cream and a grind of fresh pepper, and serve.

Deedy Marble's Red Wine Sipping Soup

Deedy Marble is the innkeeper, with her husband, Charlie, of the very excellent Governor's Inn in Ludlow, Vermont, where one winter's evening we were served the hearty and robust soup from which we adapted this one. We take a good deal of humorous pleasure in the recipe's simplicity in light of the rich taste of the finished product. Use good, hearty, inexpensive wines. We took a thermos of it skiing one day and drank it hot on a mountain-top by an icy lake, giving the children just a dram, for not all of the alcohol burns off. If you haven't made the Herbed Tomato Juice you can substitute a commercial juice.

Serves 8 to 10

1 firm winter apple, cored and quartered	4 beef bouillon cubes
1 large carrot, scraped and chunked	1 teaspoon black pepper
1 large tomato, cored and quartered	1 bottle red table wine
	1 bottle white table wine
	1 cup Herbed Tomato Juice (p. 77)

Put the apple, carrot, tomato, bouillon cubes, and pepper into the bowl of a food processor or blender and process until smooth. Pour into a stockpot, add the wines, and bring to a low boil. Boil for 35 minutes. Cool. Strain twice through several thicknesses of cheesecloth, then add the Herbed Tomato Juice. Store for up to several days in a glass bottle in the refrigerator. Serve hot, warm, or cold.

Hearty Vegetable Dishes

Wild Mushroom Lasagna

*B*UILD this dish with your own homemade pasta, to add an ethereal delicacy to the earthiness of the wild mushrooms, both brought together in a wash of tomato flavor. It's a mouth-watering dish—not difficult, but time-consuming, a good one with which to enjoy the process rather than rush through to the result. Make the tomato mushroom sauce in advance, as well as the béchamel. Be sure to allow an hour for the pasta to relax before rolling it out and assembling the dish. Take a leisurely Saturday or Sunday and make it a one-dish meal, or one to contribute to a small gathering.

> *Makes 12 first-course portions or 6 main-dish portions that melt in your mouth*

1 recipe Pasta (p. 166)

For the tomato mushroom sauce:

1 ounce dried porcini mushrooms soaked in 2 cups hot water for ½ hour	1 to 2 teaspoons fresh rosemary needles
3 tablespoons olive oil	3 pounds tomatoes, peeled, seeded, and chopped
1½ cups chopped onion	1 teaspoon salt
	a few grinds of pepper

For the béchamel:

3 tablespoons butter	4 cups milk
1 garlic clove, smashed, peeled, and minced	1 teaspoon salt
5 tablespoons flour	⅛ teaspoon ground white pepper

For the final assembly:

1 tablespoon butter	2 cups grated mozzarella
1 cup freshly grated Parmesan	

Make the pasta dough, and after it has rested for an hour, divide into four pieces and roll it in a pasta roller to #4, then cut the strip in half and continue to roll each half through to #6. The strips should then be 12 or 13 inches long, just long enough to fit into a large lasagna pan. If you're using a rolling pin, divide the dough into 8 equal pieces and roll each as thin as you can to the requisite length. Let the strips dry for at least 15 minutes.

Bring a large pot of salted water to the boil and cook 4 strips of pasta at a time for 30 seconds, tops. Place the cooked pasta in a bowl of cold water. Repeat with remaining pasta. Set the bowl of cooked pasta aside.

Make the tomato mushroom sauce: remove the mushrooms from the soaking water with a slotted spoon and chop. Strain and reserve the liquid. Heat the olive oil in a large skillet over medium heat and sauté the onion for 5 minutes. Add the rosemary, tomatoes, mushrooms, and reserved liquid and simmer 30 to 35 minutes, or until most of the liquid is evaporated. Take from the heat, stir in salt and pepper, and reserve.

Make the béchamel: melt the butter in a 1½-quart saucepan, add the garlic, and cook for 1 minute over medium heat. Whisk in the flour and cook 2 minutes until bubbling, then whisk in the milk gradually until smooth. Bring to a boil, stirring often until slightly thickened. Stir in salt and pepper and let the sauce cool.

For the final assembly: preheat the oven to 425 degrees. Butter a big, shallow baking dish (approximately 10 inches by 13 inches). Drain the noodles and blot on kitchen towels. Start by filming the bottom of the baking dish with béchamel, then begin to build the layers: (1) on the béchamel slightly overlap a layer of noodles; (2) over the noodles spread ⅓ of the tomato mushroom sauce; (3) on the sauce sprinkle a few tablespoons of the mozzarella; (4) top the mozzarella with another layer of noodles; (5) over the noodles spoon ⅓ of the béchamel; (6) over the béchamel sprinkle ⅓ of the Parmesan and a few tablespoons of the mozzarella. Repeat this process twice more from noodles through the cheeses.

At this point the lasagna can wait until you are ready to bake it, for several hours even, or it could be frozen. If so, you should let it thaw before baking it 25 to 30 minutes, until bubbling and brown on top. Let it rest at least 5 minutes before cutting.

Moroccan Vegetable Stew with Couscous

Couscous is a different and delicious grain, intriguing if you prepare it from scratch, very fast if you use the instant. Whichever you decide, this Middle Eastern vegetarian stew is a perfect mate for that grain's texture and taste.

Serves 6 to 8

¼ cup olive oil
2 cups chopped onion
2 to 3 teaspoons hot paprika or to taste
1 teaspoon cumin seeds
1 teaspoon cinnamon
½ teaspoon slightly crushed caraway seeds
1 teaspoon salt
¼ teaspoon freshly ground pepper
5 large tomatoes, coarsely chopped (5 cups)

1 sweet potato, peeled and cut in ½-inch cubes
2 tablespoons honey
1 pound zucchini, cubed
1 15-ounce can chickpeas, drained and rinsed
2 tablespoons each finely chopped parsley and cilantro
1 14-ounce package couscous prepared according to package directions

Heat oil in a large, heavy-bottomed pot over medium heat and sauté the onion with paprika, cumin, cinnamon, caraway, salt, and pepper for about 5 minutes, stirring, until the onion wilts. Add tomatoes, potato, honey, and ½ cup of water, cover, and cook 15 minutes. Add zucchini and chickpeas, cover, and cook until the vegetables are tender. Stir in the parsley and cilantro and correct seasonings. Prepare the couscous and mound in the center of a deep serving platter. Spoon vegetables and sauce around it.

Salsa Casserole with Corn Tortillas

Children as well as adults will love this easily assembled supper dish. Serve with lots of extra salsa—we recommend Dale's—and sour cream.

Serves 4 to 6

½ cup sour cream
12 corn tortillas (1
    10-ounce package)
1 pound refried beans
    (canned is okay)
3 cups Dale's Salsa
    (p. 108)

3 cups (6 ounces)
    coarsely shredded
    Monterey Jack,
    cheddar, or Colby
    cheese

Heat oven to 350 degrees. Spread 3 tablespoons of the sour cream on the bottom of a 10-inch round, shallow baking dish, gratin dish, or pie plate. Layer a fan of 4 tortillas on the sour cream, then ⅓ of the beans, ⅓ of the salsa, and ⅓ of the cheese. Repeat the layering twice more, using all of the ingredients, making sure to cover the tortillas completely to prevent them from drying out during baking.

Bake 45 minutes, take the casserole from the oven, and set it aside for a few minutes before cutting in wedges to serve with extra salsa and sour cream.

Side Dishes

Best Vermont Baked Beans

NO Vermonter could write a recipe for baked beans without sweetening them with pure Vermont maple syrup, which really is the best! Salt retards the arrival of bean tenderness, so add it toward the end of the baking.

Makes 2 quarts

1 pound dry beans—
    Great Northern,
    Yellow-Eyed, Navy,
    Baby Limas—your
    favorite or a
    combination, soaked
    (p. 160)
1 meaty ham bone
2 large ripe tomatoes,
    crushed (2 cups)
1½ cups chopped onion

½ cup pure Vermont
    maple syrup
1 tablespoon prepared
    mustard
1 bay leaf
1 tablespoon fresh
    thyme leaves or
    1 teaspoon dried
1½ teaspoons salt
¼ teaspoon freshly
    ground pepper

Preheat oven to 350 degrees. Drain and rinse beans. Place all ingredients except salt and pepper in a large, ovenproof Dutch oven, add 4 cups of cold water, cover, and bring to a boil over medium heat. Place in the oven and bake for 2 hours, after which time the mostly tender beans will have absorbed all the liquid. Add the salt and pepper, stir in 2 cups of hot water, and bake an-

Huevos Rancheros

Eggs and tomatoey beans, spicy this time. Serve with plenty of hot corn tortillas to mop the plate.

Serves 6

¼ **pound chorizo sausage, diced**
6 **corn tortillas**
5 **cups chile beans, heated through**
6 **eggs**
⅔ **cup grated Monterey Jack cheese**

Heat oven to 400 degrees. Brown the chorizo in a sauté pan and drain on a paper towel. Grease a large, shallow casserole — 7 inches by 11 inches will do — and overlap tortillas to cover the bottom. Spread the beans over the tortillas and sprinkle with the chorizo. With the back of a spoon, make 6 nests in the beans and break an egg into each nest. Sprinkle with cheese and bake just until the eggs are set but yolks are still soft, about 18 minutes.

other hour, uncovered, until beans are tender. Take from the oven, remove the bone, cut off the lean ham, shred it, and stir it back into the beans. Serve warm.

Chile Beans

In addition to the chiles below you *could* try the flavorful but very hot habanero—or try adding several of the mild dried New Mexican peppers for pure pepper flavor without much additional hotness. The chipotles will give a smoky hotness to the beans. (See our notes on chile peppers on p. 17.) This recipe makes about 10 cups of beans, which can be eaten as they are or used in various preparations such as Huevos Rancheros.

2 **tablespoons vegetable oil**
1 **cup chopped onion**
1 **teaspoon chopped garlic**
1 **bay leaf**
1 **teaspoon oregano**
1 **teaspoon ground cumin**
½ **teaspoon ground coriander**
3 **large ripe tomatoes, quartered**
2 **chipotles and 1 ancho chile, soaked in ½ cup water for ½ hour**
1 **pound dried pinto beans, soaked (p. 160)**
salt and pepper

Heat the oil in a large pot over medium heat and sauté the onion, garlic, bay leaf, oregano, cumin, and coriander for 5 minutes. Puree the tomatoes with the chiles and soaking liquid in the bowl of a food processor and add to the pot. Drain and rinse beans and stir them into the pot. Bring to a boil, lower heat, and cook partially covered until beans are tender, about 1½ hours, adding a little water if needed during cooking. Season with salt and pepper to taste.

Midwestern Kraut Tomato Bake

Before the tomatoes totally disappear from windowsills and cellar, an old northern European-cum-midwestern baked kraut with tomatoes and bacon may resurrect itself from my childhood. Sweet and sour, it is smoky and particularly good when made with homemade sauerkraut, although it's probably even more authentic when canned tomatoes and kraut are used. It is an unexpectedly beautiful dish, with jeweled tones, baking a long time in a low oven, so plan to bake meats or breads at the same time.

Laurie Colwin details a similarly transformed dish of just tomatoes sprinkled with chopped garlic and olive oil and baked in a moderate oven for a long time, until thick, browned, and very savory.

Serves 6 to 8

2 cups canned tomatoes with juice (14 ounces)	**1 cup sugar**
	¼ teaspoon salt
	several grinds of pepper
2½ cups sauerkraut (16 ounces)	**½ cup bacon cut in ½-inch pieces**

Preheat oven to 325 degrees. Mix tomatoes and sauerkraut in an oblong baking dish, 8 inches by 13 inches, breaking up the tomatoes with your fingers. A child would love this job. Pour the sugar over the mixture, sprinkle on the salt and pepper, and stir. Sprinkle the bacon over all and bake for 2¼ hours.

Light Suppers

Omelette with Fall Mushrooms

$\mathcal{W}$E often give in to the craving for the yin and yang of egg and tomato, adding a touch of cream and the wildness of mushrooms to make it perfection. Pinching bits of butter into the un-cooked eggs produces a delightfully rich dish, but you can omit it, and you can even cook with olive oil in place of butter, as little as possible for a lower-fat dish. We think that since wild mushrooms don't come along that often, we'll splurge. You can use tame mushrooms instead of wild, but the thrill will definitely be diminished.

Serves 3 to 4

For the sauce:

1 tablespoon butter
1 garlic clove, smashed,
   peeled, and minced
1 large shallot, peeled
   and minced
½ pound fresh fall
   mushrooms, cleaned
   (p. 188)

2 small ripe tomatoes,
   halved, seeded, and
   chopped (1 cup)
approximately ½ cup
   whole milk or cream

For the omelette:

6 to 8 large eggs
3 teaspoons softened
    butter
salt and pepper
1 teaspoon chopped
    fresh herbs—
    marjoram, chives,
    thyme, tarragon, or
    chervil

butter for the pan
chopped parsley
    (optional)

Make the sauce: melt the butter in a small sauté pan and sauté the garlic and shallot in it until transparent. Tear the cleaned mushrooms into it and cook over medium heat until they've given off their juice. Add the tomatoes and cook just until they give off their juice, then whisk in the cream to desired consistency.

Make the omelette: in a large bowl beat the eggs just until smooth and not stringy. Beat in bits of the butter. There will be small bits throughout the egg. Season with salt and pepper and stir in the herbs. You can make one large omelette or three small ones. Choose the size of pan you need, spray it with a vegetable cooking spray, and put it over medium-high heat. When it is hot, toss a bit of butter into the pan and, for individual omelettes, ladle in ⅓ of the egg mixture, giving it a brief stir before doing so. Shake the pan lightly to keep the omelette unstuck. When it has cooked a moment, lift up the edges of the egg and allow the un-cooked portion to run underneath. Keep shaking. When the egg is no longer runny but not quite set, shake and tilt the pan to roll the omelette over on itself. Turn the folded omelette over with a spatula, then lift out onto a warmed plate. Spoon the mushroom tomato sauce over and around. Garnish with chopped parsley if you wish and serve immediately.

Tomato, Cheddar, and Ale Sandwich

Cheese classics have a great affinity for tomato. Macaroni with cheese is all the better for the addition of a raw tomato dice folded in, and even better if shards of fresh onion are sprinkled on top. When our children were young, "grilled cheeses and Campbell's Tomato Soup" were standard fare.

It took a lot of urging for Ruth to include ale in this recipe, for she hates beer, but she loved this mellow, cheesy sauce, reminiscent of a ploughman's lunch. Of course, we use extra-sharp Vermont cheddar. Cabot cheddar is widely available and very good, and other Vermont cheeses such as Grafton, Shelburne Farms, or Crowley, my personal favorite, are wonderful if you can find them.

Serves 2

1 teaspoon butter	1 tablespoon unsalted
1 tablespoon vegetable	butter
oil	1 tablespoon flour
4 slices of good country	⅓ cup ale (Molson's)
rye bread with	⅔ cup milk
caraway seeds	1½ cups shredded
2 large ripe, juicy	Vermont extra-sharp
tomatoes, cut into 8	cheddar (3 ounces)
thick slices	½ teaspoon salt
	pinch of dry mustard

Melt the butter with the oil and brush on both sides of the bread slices. Grill or toast on a griddle until brown. Place 2 slices of bread on each of 2 plates and top with 4 tomato slices per plate.

Make the sauce: melt the butter in a small pan, stir in the flour, and cook for 1 minute. Whisk in the ale and milk and bring to a boil, stirring often. Cook until smooth and thickened, about 5 minutes, and remove from the heat. Add the cheese, salt, and mustard, and stir until smooth. Spoon the sauce over the tomatoes and serve at once.

Scalloped Potato, Ham, and Tomato Casserole

This is an old standby in our house—just creamy potatoes and succulent ham seasoned with garlic and onion, tanged by tomato and mellowed by cream and cheese, all scalloped together, and since I seldom peel a potato it's easy, too. Be sure to use starchy russet potatoes rather than the small waxy ones, because the starch absorbs these flavors better. As for cheese, I prefer a ripe, nicely melting raclette, but when it is difficult to find, as it sometimes is, use Gruyère, or even Italian fontina.

Serves 6

2½ pounds very good russet potatoes, scrubbed, sliced ¼-inch thick lengthwise, and reserved in cold water

⅔ cup finely chopped onion

1 garlic clove, smashed, peeled, and minced

⅓ jalapeño pepper (or to taste), minced

8 ounces good, lean country ham cut in ½-inch cubes (if using real Smithfield-type country ham or prosciutto, use thinly shaved slices)

2 large tomatoes, cored, halved, and chopped (2 cups)

salt and freshly ground pepper

8 ounces raclette, Gruyeré, or other Swiss cheese, shredded

1 cup heavy cream

Butter an oblong glass baking dish, 8½ inches by 13 inches. Preheat the oven to 350 degrees. Put the onion, garlic, and jalapeño in a small bowl and toss. Bring a large pot of salted water to a boil. Drain the potato slices and plunge them into the boiling water. Cover, lower heat to medium, and cook 4 minutes or until potatoes are partially tender. Drain in a colander and rinse with cold water. When slightly cooled, place a layer of them in the bottom of the baking dish. Sprinkle with the onion mixture, the ham, and half of the tomatoes. Layer the rest of the potatoes attractively, sprinkle with the rest of the tomatoes, and season with salt and freshly ground pepper. Sprinkle with the cheese. Pour the cream over and cut through the layers with a table knife in half a dozen places to allow the cream to permeate the dish. Cover with foil, tenting it if necessary so that it does not touch the cheese, and bake for 30 minutes. Remove the foil and bake until the top is browned and the potatoes are tender, 15 to 25 minutes. Serve hot or warm.

Linda's Cabbage Patch Stew

Good, quick, and uncomplicated, a kind of midwestern chile that our friend Linda Hardin Johnson brought back from a visit to her Ohio family. The potatoes are mashed and dolloped on top. It is, in one form or another, a favorite of community cookbooks.

Makes 4 to 6 servings

4 tablespoons vegetable oil
1 pound lean ground chuck
4 medium onions, halved and sliced lengthwise
2 cups shredded cabbage
1 cup diced celery
2 15-ounce cans red kidney beans, drained
2 cups cooked or canned tomatoes
2 teaspoons chile powder
salt and pepper
4 pounds all-purpose potatoes, peeled and quartered
2 tablespoons sour cream

Heat the oil in a large skillet. Brown the meat, breaking up clumps with a fork. Add onions, cabbage, and celery and cook over medium heat until wilted, about 10 minutes.

Add 4 cups of water and simmer for 15 minutes. Add beans, tomatoes, chile powder, salt, and pepper and cook 15 to 25 minutes, until thickened.

Meanwhile, cook potatoes in boiling salted water until tender. Drain, reserving about 1 cup of the cooking liquid. Mash potatoes with reserved liquid, stir in sour cream, and season with salt and pepper. Serve the stew in bowls topped with scoops of the mashed potato.

Hungarian Barley Casserole

Serve this as a light supper with a crisp salad of bitter leaves and an astringent dressing. Country bread—how about our Tomato Pumpernickel (p. 234)?—can be good with it. Serve sour cream on the side. We have access to smoky Chilean mushrooms, morels, and shiitakes and have even used regular dried button mushrooms, which are widely available but are not as flavorful as we like. Dried mushrooms usually have more intense flavors than fresh, and in this recipe we strive for intensity.

Serves 8 as a main course

¾ ounce dried mushrooms	4 cups finely chopped cabbage
4 ounces bacon, cut in ¼-inch strips	1 tablespoon sweet Hungarian paprika
1 cup coarsely chopped onion	1 cup barley
2 garlic cloves, minced	1 pound coarsely chopped tomatoes
1 cup coarsely chopped green pepper	1 teaspoon salt
	¼ teaspoon pepper

Soak mushrooms in 4 cups of hot water for ½ hour or until softened. Remove with a slotted spoon, straining the liquid through a paper towel and reserving. Then rinse and chop the mushrooms fine and set aside.

Render the bacon in a large Dutch oven over medium heat, then stir in the onion, garlic, pepper, cabbage, and paprika. Cook, stirring occasionally, for 8 to 10 minutes until vegetables are wilted. Stir in barley, tomatoes, salt, pepper, reserved mushrooms, and soaking liquid. Bring to a boil, then lower heat and simmer for 30 minutes or until the barley is tender and most of the liquid is absorbed.

Mussels in Tomato Sauce with Saffron Rice

"The subject is tomatoes," we told our friend Carol Macleod about the tomato dinner we mentioned before. "Could you do something with mussels, in a thin, winy, tomatoey, briny broth if possible?" She went home and got busy and when she came into the kitchen on the night in question with the pot of mussels in sauce, a testing finger told me it was sublime, based on a long-simmered, succulent broth made from lobster carcasses. In duplicating Carol's efforts, I added saffron rice in unconscious tribute to paella.

As for the mussels, if there's time, I like to put them in a large container, cover them with fresh water, sprinkle cornmeal over, and let them cleanse and sweeten themselves for at least an hour, then scrub and debeard them. John Thorne, on the other hand, believes that unless you have genuine seawater you will lose the briny delights of shelled things by soaking them.

If you have any sauce left over, simmer a pork roast in it in the Spanish and Portuguese style. Lamb shanks are delectable cooked in it, too.

Serves 4 to 6

For the mussels:

1 cup olive oil
3 pounds mussels, scrubbed and beards removed
1 medium onion, finely diced (or 2 large leeks, quartered lengthwise, and cut into ½-inch lengths)
3 garlic cloves, smashed, peeled, and chopped
4 cups Lobster Broth
4 cups inexpensive dry red table wine
7 ripe tomatoes, chopped (5 cups)

Lobster or Fish Broth

Often you can obtain lobster bodies (also called racks or carcasses), very cheaply, from fish stores that cook and sell lobster preparations, or you can collect and freeze the debris of your own lobster dinners until you have enough to make broth. It is best to make a large quantity on a day when windows can be opened, because, although its flavor is unsurpassed, it smells quite strongly fishy. It may be reduced to a syrup for easier storage and then reconstituted as needed.

Makes 5 to 6 cups

4 pounds lobster bodies
1 medium onion or 2 large leeks, chunked
1 medium carrot, chunked
3 bay leaves
2 stalks of lovage or 4 stalks of celery, chopped

Throw the lobster bodies into a large pot with the onion, carrot, bay leaves, and lovage or celery. Cover with 10 to 12 cups of water and bring to a boil, lower heat, and simmer until the water/broth is reduced by half or broth is of desired strength. Strain well. Use, or freeze for future use.

You can substitute fish heads and bones or shrimp shells for the lobster bodies in the recipe above; but, truth be told, I often use a Knorr's fish bouillon cube with 2 cups of water, or 1 cup of chicken broth and 1 cup of water. Or use bottled clam broth diluted or not with water.

For the rice:

1 cup basmati or other long-grain rice	2 tablespoons Lobster Broth (not hot)
1 teaspoon salt	1 bunch of parsley
¼ teaspoon saffron threads	

Heat a large, heavy skillet over medium heat, and when it is hot pour in ½ cup of the olive oil and immediately add the mussels, being careful about splatters. Shaking the pan, cook until shells open, a matter of minutes. With sturdy tongs, remove each mussel as it opens, draining any juice from the mussels back into the pan, and set them aside, discarding any that do not open. Strain the pan juices through two layers of cheesecloth or a coffee filter to eliminate any sand and grit, and reserve. Wipe the skillet out with a paper towel and put it back on the heat, add the rest of the olive oil, and sauté the onion and garlic until translucent and soft. Add the Lobster Broth, the wine, and the tomatoes and simmer until the vegetables and broth have become one, and the resulting sauce is reduced to a pleasing strength, ½ hour to 45 minutes. Add the reserved mussel juices to the sauce and barely simmer over low heat.

In the meantime, make the rice: bring 2 cups of water to a boil. Add the rice and salt, stir, cover, turn heat to very low, and simmer for 20 minutes without uncovering. Soften saffron in the 2 tablespoons of Lobster Broth and set aside. When the rice has absorbed most of the cooking water, add the saffron and broth, tossing lightly with a fork until the saffron has turned the rice yellow. Then let the rice continue to absorb the liquid over low heat until it is quite dry. Chop the parsley.

To serve, return the mussels, still in their shells, to the sauce and cook for 1 minute just to reheat. Mound ½ cup of rice in the middle of each soup plate. Surround with mussels, spoon sauce over the mussels, sprinkle with parsley, and serve immediately.

215

Tomato Hash

The word "leftover" is sadly maligned, for a well-made hash is good enough to roast a joint for. Good cooks always plan to have leftovers to turn into dishes that are as attractive as the original. Cooked mushrooms and peppers would give individuality to this dish. The food processor comes in handy in preparation.

Serves 4

2 cups leftover pork, beef, or lamb roast or combination
2 large potatoes, scrubbed, shredded, rinsed in several changes of cold water, and dried by twisting in a towel
vegetable cooking spray
1 tablespoon vegetable oil
2 large tomatoes, cored and chopped (2 cups)
½ large onion, minced
1 teaspoon dried oregano
salt and pepper
1 cup shredded cheddar or other cheese

Chop the meat fine in the bowl of a food processor fitted with the metal blade, pulsing carefully. Don't make a paste. Reserve. Spray a medium-sized frying pan with the vegetable cooking spray and place over medium heat. Add 1 tablespoon oil, tipping it over the bottom of the pan. Press in the shredded potatoes and press the chopped meat over them. Sprinkle with tomatoes, onion, and any leftovers you might desire, such as mushrooms or peppers. Sprinkle with oregano, salt, and a grind of pepper. Cover and cook over medium heat until potatoes are browned on the bottom, about 20 minutes. Sprinkle with the cheese and place under the broiler until the top is browned.

Variation: Instead of topping with cheese, you could make four nests in the hash with the back of a large spoon, then break an egg into each and sprinkle a bit of cheese over before running under the broiler. Serve in the pan.

Main Dishes

Chestnut Stuffed Cabbage

*T*HIS stuffed cabbage in the French tradition provides an earthily elegant supper. Flat leaves are lined in layers with chestnuts and ham and lean pork, spiced with marjoram and thyme, the whole braised with a tomato sauce and long baked.

The baking dish is important, for it must do dual baking and serving duty. There are many steps here, so plan on making this ahead of time or as a contribution to a potluck. At the end of baking, if you must uncover the dish to let some of the juices evaporate, use a piece of aluminum foil to cover the cabbage itself to make sure it stays its beautiful pale green, letting the juices evaporate from around the cabbage and the dish. You may use dried chestnuts—in which case remember to allow time for them to reconstitute—or whole fresh ones, baked and peeled.

Serves 10 to 12

For the sauce:

¼ cup olive oil
2 garlic cloves, smashed, peeled, and chopped
2 large shallots, chopped
4 cups chopped tomatoes
¼ cup sugar
4 tablespoons red wine vinegar
1 teaspoon salt
several grinds of pepper
1 cup rich meat broth— veal, beef, or pork

For the stuffing:

½ pound cooked, peeled
    chestnuts

5 ounces country ham,
    cut in small dice or
    chopped

12 ounces lean ground
    pork

2 onions, finely chopped

2 garlic cloves, smashed,
    peeled, and chopped

1 teaspoon crumbled
    dried marjoram

1 teaspoon dried thyme

1 teaspoon crumbled dry
    sage

1 teaspoon salt (or to
    taste)

1 teaspoon freshly
    ground pepper

2 eggs

To assemble:

a 3-pound cabbage,
    whole

2 tablespoons
    shortening, preferably
    lard

To make the sauce: heat a large, low saucepan over medium-high heat and when it is hot pour in the olive oil. When that is wavy hot, add all at once the garlic, shallots, and tomatoes and stir-fry vigorously for 3 or 4 minutes. Turn the heat to medium low and stir in the sugar, vinegar, salt, and pepper, cover, and simmer for 20 minutes, at which time stir in the meat broth. Cover, take from the heat, and set aside.

To make the stuffing: toss all ingredients together in a large bowl until lightly amalgamated. Make a ball the size of a marble and fry it to taste for seasonings; correct them. Set aside.

To prepare the cabbage: put a large pot of water on to boil. Carefully remove the outer leaves of the cabbage and with a sharp knife cut a vee out of them to remove tough stems. Save a particularly beautiful leaf to top the casserole. Cut the core out of the remaining cabbage and separate the leaves, and when the water has come to a boil blanch all the leaves for about 10 minutes. Remove from the water carefully and drain each leaf until quite dry.

Heat oven to 375 degrees and grease a heavy 4-quart casse-role with the lard. Film the bottom with tomato sauce. Cover the sides and bottom of the casserole with the largest cabbage leaves, letting them hang over the rim of the casserole, and spread a thin layer of the stuffing on the bottom ones. Cover with more leaves, pressing them down firmly so there are no air pockets. Repeat until the stuffing is all used. Fold the side leaves over the top of the last layer of stuffing and top with the reserved beautiful cab-bage leaf, molding it down over the side leaves and tucking in the edges so that there is about a 1-inch space between the stuffed cabbage and the sides of the dish. Pour the tomato sauce around and over the cabbage. Cover the dish tightly with foil or its own cover and bake for 2½ hours, or until the stuffed cabbage can be pierced easily with a pointed knife. If there is too much liquid, take off the cover of the dish and cover the cabbage loosely with aluminum foil, allowing the juices around the cabbage to evap-orate.

Cut in wedges and serve with a potato puree and crusty bread.

Braised Chicken with Apricots

This fruity chicken would titillate the appetite of a sultan. Serve it with fragrant, soft basmati rice.

Serves 4

2 tablespoons vegetable
    oil
3½-pound frying
    chicken, quartered
1 cup chopped onion
2 large ripe tomatoes,
    peeled, seeded, and
    chopped (2 cups)
5 ounces dried apricots,
    plumped in 1 cup hot
    water for ½ hour

1 teaspoon salt
1 teaspoon hot paprika
1 teaspoon cinnamon
½ teaspoon ground
    coriander
¼ teaspoon freshly
    ground pepper
1 cup basmati rice

Heat oil in a large skillet and brown the chicken pieces on both sides over medium heat. Remove chicken from the pan and set aside. Cook the onion in the skillet until wilted, about 5 minutes, then stir in the tomatoes, apricots and soaking liquid, salt, spices, and pepper, scraping up browned bits from the bottom of the pan as you do. Return the chicken pieces to the skillet, turning them in the sauce to coat. Cover, lower heat, and simmer 25 to 30 minutes, turning the chicken once. Prepare the rice.

Skim any surface fat from the sauce and correct the seasoning. Serve immediately over the cooked rice.

Pan Chicken with Tomato Hot Tarragon Sauce

If you've made the Tomato Hot Tarragon Jam with an eye to breakfast corn cakes, make it a little spicier for this dish by adding more hot pepper and/or herb to the sauce. It is best if you succeed in keeping a good crust on the chicken. Creating a succulent supper in a pan can crown a day or even a season. Make it a double tomato dinner by stirring 3 or 4 chopped dried tomatoes into the rice cooking water.

Serves 4

½ cup flour
1 teaspoon each salt and pepper
1 tablespoon each butter and olive oil
4 chicken leg and thigh quarters
1 onion
4 garlic cloves, smashed, peeled, and chopped
2 long green or red New Mexican peppers, dried or fresh, halved and seeded

1 sweet red pepper, quartered and seeded
1 cup Rich Chicken Broth (p. 116)
1 cup inexpensive dry red table wine
½ cup Tomato Hot Tarragon Jam (p. 151)
1 teaspoon flour mashed into 1 teaspoon butter to make a beurre manié
1 cup basmati rice

Heat a large sauté pan over medium heat. Mix flour, salt, and pepper on a large piece of waxed paper. Dredge the chicken quarters in the seasoned flour. When the pan is hot, add the butter and the oil, and when the butter is melted, brown the chicken quarters on one side over medium heat, shaking the pan often, until they are dark golden brown and very crusty, then turn them and brown the other side. Take your time and take care not to let them burn as they develop a crust that will not turn to mush in the sauce. Add more oil if needed. Peel and quarter the onion, but leave most of the root end intact to hold each segment together. When the chicken is browned, poke the vegetables down into the pan between the chicken pieces and add a bit of the Chicken Broth to steam and soften the vegetables. Cook until the chicken is tender, turning it back on its first side if need be, and the vegetables are crisp/tender, ½ to ¾ hour altogether, then remove the chicken pieces and vegetables to a platter. Keep them warm while you cook the rice and prepare the sauce.

Reduce any pan juices over medium-high heat until they are caramelized on the bottom of the pan and the fat is transparent over the top. Pour off the fat and discard, then pour in the wine and remaining Chicken Broth, scraping the caramelized juices from the bottom of the pan until they meld with the broth. Simmer until slightly thickened, then stir in the jam and simmer 5 minutes. Whisk bits of the beurre manié into the sauce until it is smooth and satiny. Put the chicken back into the pan, place vegetables on top, cover, and heat just until warmed through.

Serve immediately over the cooked rice.

Grilled Shrimp with Tomato Hot Tarragon Jam

Simple to do, these are the perfect hors d'oeuvres for any season and a fine main course for a hot summer's day. Serve them with our nutty multigrain Tabbouleh (p. 125).

Serves 4 as a main course and 16 as an hors d'oeuvre

32 large shrimp, peeled	**½ cup Tomato Hot**
¼ cup lime juice	**Tarragon Jam**
1 teaspoon salt	**(p. 151)**
	lime wedges

Marinate the shrimp in the lime juice and salt for 1 hour. Heat the grill. Drain the shrimp and divide them among 4 metal skewers. Melt the jam with 2 tablespoons of water in a small saucepan over medium heat and brush it on the skewered shrimp. Brush the grill with oil and cook the shrimp 2 to 3 minutes on each side or until pink and opaque. Do not overcook. Garnish with lime wedges and serve any remaining jam as a dip.

Ragout of Duck Legs with Green Olives

Shards of rosemary and slices of big green Sicilian olives mingle aromatically in this sauce in which the duck legs are braised. With 1 duck, this makes an elegant supper for 2. Use 2 ducks for 4 people. Polenta, allowed to cool, then sliced and fried in a bit of the rendered duck fat before being allowed to soak up a bit of the duck juices, would be quite delicious here. It would also go well with homemade noodles or kasha. What with boning the ducks, making the broth, and then marinating the duck legs overnight, this is a lengthy recipe, but none of the steps is difficult and the finished product is very worthwhile.

Serves 4

4 duck leg and thigh quarters	2 tablespoons duck fat skimmed from the broth
1 to 2 teaspoons fresh rosemary needles	8 Sicilian green olives, pitted and sliced
1 large garlic clove, chopped	2 large ripe tomatoes, peeled, seeded, and chopped (2 cups)
1 cup dry white wine	1 cup Duck Broth
½ teaspoon salt	
⅛ teaspoon freshly ground pepper	

Make a marinade of the rosemary, garlic, wine, salt, and pepper, and pour it over the duck legs in a glass dish. Cover and refrigerate overnight.

When ready to cook, drain the duck pieces and reserve the marinade. Heat the duck fat in a large skillet over medium heat. Dry the duck pieces with paper towels, sprinkle with salt and pepper, and brown on both sides, then remove the legs and discard any fat accumulated in the pan. Return the duck to the pan, strew the olives around, add tomatoes, broth, and reserved marinade, and bring to a boil. Then lower heat, cover, and simmer 35 to 40 minutes until the duck is tender. Remove the pieces to a platter and keep them warm as you skim off any surface fat from the

How to Bone a Duck

Remove the wing tips and second wing joints from the duck. Cut down the middle of the breastbone and separate breasts by running the knife between the meat and the bone, toward the wing. The breasts will lift off in one piece. Cut off excess skin and fat and render, if you like, or discard. To remove the legs, lift leg in one hand, then run knife through inside thigh joint where it joins the carcass. Reserve the leg and thigh quarters and the breasts. Chop the carcass into 2-inch pieces to make a broth.

Duck Broth

giblets (except the liver),
chopped carcasses, wing tips,
and second wing joints of
2 ducks, 4 to 5 pounds each
1 onion, halved through stem
end, unpeeled
3 cloves garlic, unpeeled
1 carrot, peeled and quartered

Preheat oven to 450 degrees. Place duck parts and vegetables in a roasting pan large enough to accommodate them in one layer and roast for 30 minutes or until very brown. Remove to a pot with a slotted spoon or a Chinese sieve. Spoon off the fat from the roasting pan and reserve. Deglaze the roasting pan with 1 cup of water, scrape up any brown bits, and add to the pot with 6 cups of water. Bring to a boil over medium heat, lower heat, and simmer for about 2 hours, then strain through a fine-mesh sieve or towel. You should have about 2 cups of broth. Cool and remove any fat that hardens on the surface.

sauce, raise the heat, and reduce it by half. To serve, spoon the sauce over the duck legs.

Duck Breasts in Figgy Tomato Sauce

Figs are one of our favorite fruits. Fresh ones, though scarce, are such a treat they demand only a bit of cream or the salt of prosciutto when they are available. In this recipe, we use dried figs for their concentrated sugars and flavors, immersing a dozen big, plump, golden Calimyrnas in marsala, sherry, or brandy to cover, and letting them steep for a day, a week, or a year. The liquor and the fruit merge, over time, into a complexity of flavor and aroma, the liquor becoming thick with fig flavor, and the figs ready to be retrieved, quartered, and used with a little of their liquor in various meat and dessert sauces—or on their own, broiled for a moment and served around a mound of Crème Fraîche (p. 56), accompanied by a rich shortbread or sugar cookie.

In this recipe, the figs with their liquor combine wonderfully with the tomatoes to create a fully pungent whole. Try this sauce also with sautéed calf's liver.

Serves 4

4 duck breasts
1 tablespoon rendered
  duck fat or olive oil
salt and freshly ground
  pepper
¼ cup minced shallots
¼ cup dry red wine
1½ cups Duck Broth or
  Rich Chicken Broth
  (p. 116)

1 large ripe tomato,
  peeled, seeded, and
  chopped (1 cup)
6 figs soaked in sherry,
  drained and
  quartered (see above)
¾ cup sherry

Place the duck breasts skin side down on a cutting board and carefully separate the meat from the skin, leaving the skin attached at the long edge of the breast. With a very sharp knife, scrape away as much fat from the skin as possible without tear-

225

ing it. Smooth the skin back over the breast and prick all over with the tip of the knife. Pat the breasts dry with paper towels and sprinkle the meat side with salt and pepper.

Heat a 12-inch skillet over high heat, add the fat or the olive oil, and sear the breasts, skin side down. Lower heat to medium and cook about 5 minutes until skin is browned and crisp. Turn and cook the other side for 4 to 5 minutes. The breasts will be pink in the center. Remove them to a platter and cover loosely with foil while you make the sauce.

Discard all but 1 tablespoon of fat from the pan and stir the shallots into the fat. Cook for 1 minute, stirring often. Deglaze the pan with the wine, scraping up the browned bits from the bottom. Add the broth and let boil and reduce for about 12 minutes or until only about ½ cup of the liquid remains. Stir in the tomato, figs, sherry, and any accumulated juices from the reserved breasts. Bring to a boil, then lower the heat to a simmer for 10 minutes. Season to taste with salt and pepper.

To serve, slice each breast on the diagonal in 5 or 6 slices and overlap on a serving plate. Spoon the sauce over and around each breast.

Basque Style Spicy Lobster

Ruth fell in love with a similar dish served by a favorite restaurant in Newark, New Jersey, home to many Basque, Spanish, and Portuguese Americans. She reconstructs it here. Serve it with rice.

Serves 4

4 lobsters, 1 to
   1¼ pounds each
3 tablespoons olive oil
1 cup sliced onion
2 large garlic cloves,
   smashed, peeled, and
   minced
1 large red pepper, cut
   in strips

½ small dried hot
   pepper, chopped, or
   ¼ teaspoon crushed
   red pepper flakes
4 large ripe tomatoes,
   chopped (4 cups)
salt and pepper to taste

Heat a large pot of water to boiling, and plunge the lobsters in headfirst. Cover and cook 3 minutes. Remove lobsters with long-handled tongs and cool briefly. Over a large bowl, break the claws and tail from the body, catching all the juices and the tomalley in the bowl. Reserve the carcasses to be frozen and made into broth in the future. Crack the claws with kitchen shears, a nutcracker, or the side of a heavy cleaver. Cut tails in half lengthwise.

Heat the oil in a 12-inch skillet over medium-high heat and sauté the onion, garlic, and sweet and hot peppers until they're wilted, about 7 minutes. Add the tomatoes and let simmer for 20 to 30 minutes or until the mixture thickens, then add the lobster pieces and all the reserved juices to the skillet. Raise the heat to high and cook for 5 minutes, stirring often. Salt and pepper to taste. Serve with rice.

Saltfish Curry

A savory way to treat salt cod, which used to be a staple of many New England states, when it was often served, creamed, over potatoes. As with dried mushrooms, the flavor of cod is made complex, the texture silken, by drying. Our adventurous seasonings call for rice, and we recommend basmati.

Serves 4

1 pound dried boneless cod, soaked overnight in several changes of cold water
1 teaspoon cumin seeds
½ teaspoon mustard seeds
½ teaspoon coriander seeds
seeds from 6 cardamom pods
1 small dried hot pepper
½ teaspoon salt
¼ teaspoon freshly ground pepper

2 tablespoons vegetable oil
1 tablespoon butter
1 tablespoon minced garlic
2 tablespoons minced gingerroot
2 tablespoons lime juice
3 cups crushed tomatoes
1 cup basmati rice
2 tablespoons minced scallions

Drain the fish, cut into 2-inch cubes, and set aside.

In a small skillet toast the cumin, mustard, coriander, and cardamom seeds and the hot pepper for several minutes over low heat until they are fragrant, being careful not to burn them. Grind with the salt and pepper until powdered. Heat the oil and butter in a 2-quart casserole over medium heat, and sauté the spices, garlic, and gingerroot for 3 minutes. Toss in the cod to coat with the spice mixture. Add the lime juice and tomatoes, bring to a simmer, cover, lower heat, and cook 20 to 25 minutes.

Prepare the rice.

When fish is tender, sprinkle with scallions and serve.

Tomato Swiss Steak Courcelle

Vegetables and the whiter meats are delicious, and healthy, too, and they are almost all we want in the warmer weather, but for some people there is nothing like the aroma of a long and gently cooked bit of red meat to warm a chilly house in a blowzy month like November.

It's a lovely thing to have a pair of personable butchers in your own village. I was thinking about Swiss steak one day when I walked into the Wallingford Locker. Even my *Larousse Gastronomique* did not explain what the term "Swiss" meant.

"Long braised, covered, in a red sauce," said Paul Courcelle, one of the butchers, adding that I needn't look for a tender cut. His brother Justin intervened. "Let me give you some chuck," he said, offering the fact that his wife, Gale, had a "great" recipe for Swiss steak in the *Vermont Symphony Cookbook*, one of my favorites. He cut some beautiful little chuck cutlets, as many as he knew would feed my family, and put them neatly on the green paper on the scale, looking at me questioningly. I nodded, he wrapped them up, and I went home and followed Gale's recipe, modifying it slightly to fit my own family. But it's Gale's balance of seasonings here that is so fine. Serve it with good mashed potatoes.

Serves 4

3 tablespoons vegetable oil
1 garlic clove, smashed, peeled, and minced
1 cup sliced onion
¾ cup flour
2½ teaspoons salt
2 teaspoons pepper
1½ pounds lean chuck, cut into 2-inch by 3-inch cutlets

2 large tomatoes, chopped, or 2 cups canned
1 cup red table wine
1 tablespoon Worcestershire sauce
1 tablespoon dry mustard
1 tablespoon brown sugar
1 tablespoon paprika

In a large skillet heat the oil over medium heat and sauté the garlic and the onion until browned, stirring often. In the meantime, season the flour with 1 teaspoon each of the salt and pepper on waxed paper, and dredge the meat in it, tapping off the excess. Push the onion and garlic to one side of the pan and brown the meat on both sides. In a bowl, mix the tomatoes, wine, Worcestershire, mustard, sugar, paprika, and remaining salt and pepper, and pour over the browned steak in pan. Simmer until tender, about 1½ hours.

Pot-Roasted Pork Shoulder with Tomatoes

This pot roast is fork-tender and has the most marvelous flavor. Plan to start preparations the day before serving it, as it must marinate overnight. Serve with buttered noodles.

Serves 8 to 10

5- to 6-pound pork shoulder roast	**1¼ cups sliced onion**
1 tablespoon olive oil	**6 large ripe tomatoes (3 pounds), coarsely chopped**
1 tablespoon paprika	
½ teaspoon salt	**½ teaspoon salt**
¼ teaspoon freshly ground pepper	**2 bay leaves**
	1 tablespoon flour
2 garlic cloves, smashed, peeled, and minced	**1 tablespoon unsalted butter**
1 tablespoon olive oil	

The day before serving, remove the skin of the pork roast, if it has one, and trim the fat. In a mortar or a small bowl, make a paste of the olive oil, paprika, salt, pepper, and garlic. Rub the marinade into the roast, place it in a pan or a bowl, cover, and refrigerate overnight.

Four hours before serving, bring the roast to room temperature. Place a large, heavy-bottomed pot over high heat, add the olive oil, and brown the roast on all sides for about half an hour. Add the onion, tomatoes, salt, and bay leaves to the pot, cover, lower heat, and cook gently for about 1½ hours. Turn the meat in its juices, cover, and cook until fork-tender, perhaps another hour, perhaps more. Remove the meat to a serving platter and cover to keep warm. Skim the fat from the pan juices, then turn heat to high and boil them, with lid askew, until reduced by half. Mash the flour and butter together, and add bit by bit to the simmering sauce until lightly thickened. Correct seasonings. Slice the meat and spoon the sauce over it.

Braised Lamb Shanks

Lamb shanks are succulent, gelatinous cuts of meat, recently back in favor after long neglect. This combination of spices and herbs makes a perfumed dish. Serve over fried polenta slices or homemade noodles.

Serves 4

4 lamb shanks (2½ to 3 pounds)
2 tablespoons olive oil
1 cup sliced onion
2 garlic cloves, smashed and peeled
1 bay leaf
1 cinnamon stick
1 teaspoon crushed fennel seeds
1 to 2 teaspoons fresh rosemary needles
½ teaspoon thyme leaves
1 teaspoon salt
¼ teaspoon freshly ground pepper
1 cup dry white wine
2 large ripe tomatoes, crushed (2 cups)

Brown the lamb shanks in oil on all sides in a heavy-bottomed casserole over medium-high heat. Add onion, garlic, spices, herbs, and salt and pepper. Add wine, bring to a boil, and then stir in the tomatoes. Cover, lower heat, and simmer slowly for about 2 hours. Turn the meat a couple of times during the cooking. Cook until very tender. Skim off any surface fat from the sauce and serve.

Squash Stuffed with Lamb

Pungently sweet and sour, this supper dish is informal and hearty. It could easily be doubled.

Serves 2

1 acorn or delicata
   squash, halved
   lengthwise and
   seeded
2 tablespoons olive oil
½ pound lean ground
   lamb
1 small onion, sliced
1 garlic clove, smashed,
   peeled, and chopped
¼ teaspoon salt
½ teaspoon pepper
½ teaspoon dried red
   pepper flakes

⅓ cup basmati rice
1 tablespoon fresh sage,
   chopped, or 1
   teaspoon dried
1 tablespoon pure
   Vermont maple syrup
¼ cup white wine
½ cup Sautéed Fresh
   Tomato Sauce (p. 65)
1 tablespoon toasted
   pine nuts

Preheat the oven to 350 degrees. Oil a baking dish that will hold the squash snugly, cut side down, and bake the squash 20 minutes or until a fork can easily prick the flesh. In the meantime, heat a large skillet over medium-high heat, add the oil, and break up the meat in it. Stir in the onion, garlic, salt, pepper, and dried pepper flakes. Add the rice and cook, stirring, until rice is golden, about 5 minutes. Stir in the sage, syrup, wine, ¼ cup of the tomato sauce, and ⅓ cup water. Cover and steam over low heat for 10 to 15 minutes, until the rice is just tender and has absorbed most of the liquid. Stir in the pine nuts.

Turn the squash halves over and spoon the meat filling into them, patting and mounding it. Use all the filling. Top each squash half with remaining tomato sauce. Bake another 20 minutes and serve hot.

Breads

Tomato Pumpernickel Bread

$\mathcal{W}$E are a generation that grew up on bread, a whole slice of which could be squashed down into a pellet the size of a walnut or smaller. For some of us that became the measure for bread—anything chewier, browner, or in any way more "difficult" was not fit to wrap a slice of bologna dunked in ketchup. For others of us it was a revelation the way chewy French baguettes tasted with a chunk of Vermont cheddar and a bit of sausage, or black pumpernickel with sweet butter and liver sausage, and then the search was on. It was often a futile search because good bread was practically unknown and certainly not high on the list of priorities of many. But it became more and more important as people had the opportunity to taste real bread in their travels. We are able at this point to find good bread from various local and regional bakeries, but we particularly like the chewy country sourdough loaves baked by our friends Ray and Christine Powers in the big, wood-fired brick oven in their home and bakery up on Bear Mountain. As well, Baba-a-Louis here makes wonderful bread, some sourdough. We trust that good bread is generally available throughout the United States by this time. If it is not, and even if it is, one truly satisfying source of it is our own home ovens.

This is our adaptation of big, dark bread and is based on the Vermont Bread Company's deeply good European-style Black Russian bread. It seemed the perfect thing to enclose slices of tomato and young leaves of arugula and other herbs after being slathered with mayo. It is a well-risen, soft bread, but with character, and moist enough to encompass the slices of tomatoes without falling apart. We called Lisa Lorimer at the Vermont Bread Company in Brattleboro, and she gave us a brief pumpernickel history. She told us that bakers often relied on chemicals to produce this dark, flavorful bread, but that European bakers would take the ends of other loaves, the extras left over at the end of the day, and bake them until they were crisp and burned, then make a slurry out of them to flavor the next batch of pumpernickel. In Lisa's bread the sweetness and the color come from molasses and carob—although chocolate could be used, and we use cocoa in this recipe — and Lisa is working on a way to incorporate coffee. She was kind enough to give us the proportions of ingredients she uses to make hundreds of loaves, and we got out our calculator to make two, substituting tomato puree for the liquid to provide moistness as well as flavor. This dark, mahogany-colored loaf is the perfect tomato bread, and the perfect bread for tomatoes.

Ruth says to tell you that 1 tablespoon of lightly crushed caraway seeds could be added with the flours if you so desire.

Makes 2 large loaves

1 tablespoon dried yeast
¼ cup hot water
    (120 degrees)
¼ cup dark, unsulfured
    molasses
1¾ cups all-purpose
    white flour (plus
    more for kneading)
1¾ cups whole-wheat
    flour
½ cup rye flour

2 tablespoons
    unsweetened cocoa
    powder
1 tablespoon salt
2 cups tomato puree,
    room temperature
cornmeal
1 egg white mixed with
    1 tablespoon water
    and a pinch of salt

In a large mixing bowl stir the yeast into the water and molasses and let proof for 5 minutes until the yeast bubbles. Stir in the flours, cocoa, salt, and tomato puree until the liquid is incorporated, turn out onto a flat, lightly floured work surface, and knead until smooth, about 10 minutes. The dough will be soft but not particularly sticky. Lightly grease the bowl, put the dough into it, cover with a plastic bag, and let rise in a warm, draft-free place until very light and doubled in volume, at least an hour.

Punch the dough down and divide it in half on a floured work surface. Pat each half into a rectangle and roll from the short end like a jelly roll. Pinch the seam together firmly and taper ends to form a football-shaped loaf. Lightly grease a baking sheet and sprinkle it with cornmeal. Place each loaf seam side down on the sheet, cover, and let rise until doubled in a warm, draft-free place.

Heat the oven to 375 degrees. Make three diagonal slashes across the top of each loaf with a razor. Brush with the egg white mixture and bake for 20 minutes. Brush again and continue baking for 15 to 20 minutes longer or until very brown, and the loaves sound hollow when rapped on the bottom. Let cool on a rack.

Tomato and Cracked Pepper Biscuits

Ruth was entranced by a Nova Scotian friend's memory of an aunt who made a pink biscuit using tomato juice. These turn a lovely golden orange when they are baked.

Makes 8 wedges

2 cups minus
  2 tablespoons
  all-purpose flour
2 tablespoons cornmeal
2 teaspoons baking
  powder
1 teaspoon baking soda
½ teaspoon salt

¼ teaspoon coarsely
  ground black pepper
2 tablespoons unsalted
  butter
3 tablespoons solid
  vegetable shortening
⅔ cup tomato juice

Preheat oven to 425 degrees. Mix flour, cornmeal, baking powder, baking soda, salt, and pepper together in a bowl. Cut in butter and shortening until mixture resembles oatmeal. Add tomato juice and toss mixture with a fork until it forms a ball. Turn out on a floured work surface and knead 8 to 10 times. Pat into a 7-inch circle about ½ inch thick and place on an ungreased baking sheet. Cut into 8 wedges and pull each back so that they are separated by 1 inch. Bake 15 minutes or until golden brown. Cool on a rack just briefly and serve warm with sweet butter.

Semolina Quickbread

A cakelike bread with a frill of earthy sweetness. Serve it in wedges with very thinly sliced dry ham, such as prosciutto or Smithfield, and wedges of tiny late-season melons, such as the pink-fleshed Charantais or the delicate green Israeli Perfume Gala, nestled on leaves of arugula. A perfect starter for a brunch featuring the Omelette with Fall Mushrooms (p. 207).

Serves 8 to 10

1½ cups all-purpose flour
½ cup semolina
1 tablespoon sugar
1½ teaspoons baking powder
1 teaspoon baking soda
1 teaspoon salt
¼ teaspoon freshly ground pepper
½ cup dried tomatoes packed in olive oil, drained and chopped

8 black oil-cured olives, pitted and chopped
½ cup sultanas (golden raisins)
½ cup chopped toasted walnuts
3 eggs
⅓ cup vegetable oil
1½ cups buttermilk

Preheat oven to 350 degrees. Grease a 9-inch by 2-inch round cake pan.

Combine dry ingredients in a large bowl. In another bowl toss the tomatoes, olives, raisins, and nuts and then the eggs and oil, beating with a fork to break up the eggs. Stir in the buttermilk and add to the dry ingredients. Stir only until the flour is moistened. Pour into the pan and bake 45 minutes or until golden brown, and a tester inserted in the center of the cake comes out clean. Cool in the pan for 10 minutes, then invert on a rack to finish cooling. Cut into wedges.

Desserts

Crazy Brownies

*W*HEN we were growing up, housewives exchanged an eccentric little recipe for chocolate cake made with tomato soup. No book about tomatoes would be complete without this humorous but fine-tasting technique. We've used tomato puree in these moist, caky, chocolaty brownies.

Makes 16 squares

1 cup packed light
    brown sugar
2 squares unsweetened
    chocolate
½ cup unsalted butter
¾ cup all-purpose flour
¼ cup cocoa powder
½ teaspoon cinnamon

½ teaspoon baking soda
2 eggs, lightly beaten
½ cup tomato puree (or
    Roasted Plain
    Tomato Sauce,
    p. 108)
1 cup chopped walnuts

Preheat oven to 350 degrees. Grease an 8-inch-square baking pan. Mix sugar, chocolate squares, and butter in a small saucepan and stir over low heat until the chocolate is melted and sugar is dissolved, and let cool. Stir flour, cocoa, cinnamon, and baking soda together in a small bowl. Whisk the chocolate mixture and then the tomato puree into the eggs. Stir in the flour mixture and add nuts. Scrape into the pan and bake 35 minutes or until a wooden pick inserted into the center of the brownies comes out dry. Cool in pan on a rack for 20 minutes. Cut into squares while still warm.

Old-Fashioned Tomato Raisin Dumplings

There are many tomato desserts listed in old cookbooks. After trying a Shaker recipe for tomato dumplings, we shook our heads, puzzled, thinking that our food tastes had changed irrevocably over the years. Still, we were intrigued. Out of our persistence came this treat, proving that some old-time ideas deserve another taste.

Serves 6

6 small tomatoes, peeled and cored

For the filling:

⅓ **cup raisins**
⅓ **cup packed light brown sugar**
½ **cup soft whole-wheat Bread Crumbs (p. 90)**

2 tablespoons softened unsalted butter

For the dough:

3 cups all-purpose flour
3 tablespoons sugar
1 tablespoon baking powder

¾ **teaspoon salt**
¾ **cup shortening**
1 cup milk

For the syrup:

1 cup packed light brown sugar

1 cup water
Crème Fraîche (p. 56)

Cut a cross halfway into each tomato and gently squeeze out seeds and juice. Place raisins, sugar, and Bread Crumbs in the bowl of a food processor and pulse just until the raisins are chopped. Add the butter and pulse several times until the mixture holds together. Stuff the center of each tomato with the raisin mixture and let tomatoes sit on a paper towel to absorb any excess moisture while you prepare the dough.

Heat the oven to 425 degrees. Stir flour, sugar, baking powder, and salt together in a bowl. Cut in shortening with a pastry blender until mixture resembles oatmeal. Stir in milk with a fork and gather the dough into a ball. Turn onto a lightly floured surface and knead 7 or 8 times. Roll dough thin and cut into six 6-inch squares. Place a stuffed tomato in the center of each square and seal by bringing the corners together at the top and twisting dough slightly. Pinch the seams together firmly.

Place the dumplings in a well-buttered baking dish. Mix the sugar and water together to make a syrup and pour around the dumplings. Bake for 45 minutes, or until pastry is golden brown. Serve warm with the syrup and a spoonful of Crème Fraîche.

Sweet Tomato and Bread Pudding

Peder Johnson remembered this old dish as a sweet, puddeny side dish that he had loved when served it as a child in Toledo. So he called his mother, Margaret Lewis Bitter, who gave him a list of ingredients off the top of her head and a sketchy method, and told him that its fame, as the specialty of a well-known Toledo restaurant, had spread far and wide back in the twenties. We couldn't believe it. We scratched our heads and left testing it for last, but when we did, it proved to be a luscious, caramel-tasting pudding that we would use to put a cap on any dinner rather than as a side dish. It's very simple to make with a good, chewy French-type bread. Add a spoonful of Crème Fraîche on the side.

Serves 4 to 6

1 cup packed light brown sugar	¼ cup melted unsalted butter
1 cup tomato puree	Crème Fraîche (p. 56)
2 cups cubed firm French bread	

Heat the oven to 325 degrees. Stir the sugar, tomato puree, and ¼ cup of water together in a saucepan and cook for 5 minutes over medium-low heat, stirring occasionally. Toss the bread cubes with the butter in a 1-quart ovenproof casserole. Pour the tomato mixture over the bread and let sit for 15 minutes. Bake for 50 minutes. Cool and serve small portions with spoonfuls of Crème Fraîche.

Mail-Order Sources

American Spoon Foods, Inc.
  (wild foods, dried berries,
  and mushrooms, particularly morels)
1668 Clarion Ave., P.O. Box 566
Petoskey, MI 49770–0566
(800) 222-5886

Crowley Cheese, Inc.
  (the best Colby cheese)
Rte. 103
Healdville, VT 05758

Grafton Cheese
Grafton, VT 05146

Hoppin' John's
  (culinary books and ingredients)
30 Pinckney St.
Charleston, SC 29401

Sandy and Dale Lincoln
Environ Herbal Vinegars
P.O. Box 92, Creek Road
Wallingford, VT 05773

Shep and Ellen Ogden (seeds)
Cook's Garden
P.O. Box 535
Londonderry, VT 05148
(800) 824-3400

Pomona Universal Pectin
P.O. Box 1083
Greenfield, MA 01302
(Workstead Industries: [413] 772-6816)

Chris and Ray Powers
  (sourdough breads)
Bear Mountain Bakers
Wallingford, VT 05773

Seeds of Change
1364 Rufina Circle #5
Santa Fe, NM 87501
(505) 438-8080

Shelburne Farms (cheese)
Shelburne, VT 05482

Andrew Snyder and Christine Anderson
  (flavored vinegars, maple syrup
  and confections, pickles)
Fire Hill Farm
Florence, VT 05744
(800) 69-SYRUP

Spring Lake Ranch
  (Vermont maple syrup)
Rte. 103
Cuttingsville, VT 05738

Yoder's Country Market
  (dried beans, bulk yeast, spices, flavorings)
Pratts, VA 22731

To give or receive information on tomatoes contact

Andrew Smith's Tomato History and Culture
  Project
135 Eastern Parkway, #11a
Brooklyn, NY 11238

Bibliography

BOOKS

Ball Corporation. *Ball Blue Book,* 32nd ed. Ball Corporation, Box 2005, Department WL, Muncie, IN 47307–0005.

Barron, Rosemary. *Flavors of Greece.* New York: William Morrow, 1991.

Beard, James. *Delights and Prejudices.* New York: Atheneum, 1981.

Behr, Edward. *The Artful Eater.* New York: Atlantic Monthly Press, 1992.

Child, Lydia Maria. *The American Frugal Housewife.* Boston: Carter, Hendee and Company, 1832.

David, Elizabeth. *French Provincial Cooking.* Middlesex: Penguin, 1960.

————. *An Omelet and a Glass of Wine.* Middlesex: Penguin, 1986.

DeWitt, Dave, and Nancy Gerlach. *The Whole Chile Pepper Book.* Boston: Little, Brown and Company, 1990.

DuBose, Fred. *The Total Tomato.* New York: Harper Colophon Books, 1985.

Field, Carol. *Celebrating Italy.* New York: William Morrow, 1990.

Gerard, John. *Herball.* Originally published 1636.

Gray, Patience. *Honey from a Weed.* New York: Harper and Row, 1987.

Greene, Janet. *Putting Food By* (with Ruth Hertzberg and Beatrice Vaughan). 4th ed. Lexington, MA/New York: Stephen Green Press/Penguin Books, 1988.

Johnston, Mireille. *The Cuisine of the Sun.* New York: Random House, 1979.

Kennedy, Diane. *Recipes from the Regional Cooks of Mexico.* New York: HarperCollins, 1978.

Killeen, Johanne, and George Germon. *Cucina Simpatica.* New York: HarperCollins, 1991.

Kowalchik, Claire, and William H. Hylton, eds. *Rodale's Illustrated Encyclopedia of Herbs.* Emmaus, PA: Rodale Press, 1987.

Ladies of the Golden Circle. *Crumbs from Everybody's Table: A Cookbook.* Swanton, VT: The Swanton Reporter (n.d.).

Lang, George. *The Cuisine of Hungary.* New York: Bonanza, 1971.

La Place, Viana. *Verdura.* New York: William Morrow, 1991.

Matson, Ruth A. *Cooking by the Garden Calendar.* Garden City, NY: The American Garden Guild and Doubleday & Co., Inc., 1955.

Miller, Amy Bess Williams, and Persis Wellington Fuller, eds. *The Best of Shaker Cooking.* New York: Macmillan, 1970.

Ody, Penelope. *The Complete Medicinal Herbal.* New York: Dorling Kindersley, Inc., 1993.

Romer, Elizabeth. *The Tuscan Year.* New York: Atheneum, 1985.

Rorer, Sarah Tyson. *How to Cook Vegetables*. Philadelphia: W. Atlee Burpee & Co., 1903.

Rutland Area Chapter of the Friends of VSO. *Vermont Symphony Cookbook*. Rutland, VT: Vermont Symphony Orchestra Association, 1984.

Rutledge, Sarah. *The Carolina Housewife* (facsimile of 1847 edition, with additions by Anna Wells Rutledge). Columbia, SC: University of South Carolina Press, 1979.

Smith, Andrew. *The Tomato in America: Early History, Culture and Cookery*. Columbia, SC: University of South Carolina Press, 1994.

Taylor, John Martin. *Hoppin' John's Lowcountry Cooking*. New York: Bantam, 1992.

Thorne, John. *Outlaw Cook* (with Matt Lewis Thorne). New York: Farrar, Straus & Giroux, 1992.

———. *Simple Cooking*. New York: Viking, 1987.

Walter, Eugene. *Hints & Pinches*. Atlanta: Longstreet Press, 1991.

White, Jasper. *Jasper White's Cooking from New England*. New York: HarperCollins, 1989.

ARTICLES

Coe, Sophie. "Aztec Cuisine, Part II," *Petits Propos Culinaires* 20. London: Prospect Books, 1985.

Colwin, Laurie. "Tomatoes." *Gourmet* (August 1992).

Jubera, Cynthia Hizer, and Eugene Walter. "Reel Life," *Food Arts* (July/August 1992).

Smith, Andrew F. "The Amazing Archibald Miles and His Miracle Pills: Dr. Miles' Compound Extract of Tomato," *Queen City Heritage: The Journal of the Cincinnati Historical Society* 50, no. 2 (Summer 1992): 36–48.

———. "The Making of the Legend of Robert Gibbon Johnson and the Tomato," *New Jersey History* 108 (Fall/Winter 1990): 59–74.

———. "The Rise and Fall of Home-Made Anglo-American Tomato Ketchup," *Petits Propos Culinaires* 39. London: Prospect Books, 1985.

NEWSLETTERS

The Tomato Club, by Bob Ambrose
114 East Main St.
Bogota, NJ 07603

Cook & Tell, by Karyl Bannister
Love's Cove
West Southport, ME 04576

The Art of Eating (quarterly letter), by Edward Behr
Box 242
Peacham, VT 05862

Food History News, by S. L. Oliver
HCR 81 Box 354A
Isleboro, ME 04848

Simple Cooking, by John Thorne and Matt Lewis Thorne
P.O. Box 88
Steuben, ME 04680

CookBook: The Food Book Review for Cooks Who Read (the Thornes' second publication)

Index